THEY NAMED ME MARJORIE
     § · §

೭ೲ They Named Me Marjorie ೮೪

The Brave Journey of an Orphan Train Rider

Ann Zemke

ISBN: 9779699-0-8

Pre-press by North Star Press of St. Cloud, Inc.,
P.O. Box 451, St. Cloud, Minnesota.

Printing by Versa Press, Inc., East Peoria, Illinois.

Published by:
Crocus Lane Quilts
11060 Amen Circle NE
Blaine, Minnesota 55449

www.crocuslanequilts.com
ann@crocuslanequilts.com

Dedication

Thank you, Grandma,
for the legacy of courage and strength
that you left your family.
We are eternally grateful.

ஐ Foreword ை

I N THE MID-1800s, THOUSANDS OF EMIGRANTS left their native countries and extended families to seek opportunity in young and prosperous America. When they arrived, however, they often found a life of hardship, much different from what they had expected. Despite the industrial revolution, jobs were scarce for the huge numbers of immigrants flooding into the country. If they were able to find work, they worked long, hard hours for minimal pay in dangerous working conditions. Food was scarce. Often both parents needed to work but lacked the extended family to care for their children. Industrial accidents took the lives of many workers, and single-parent families were forced to the streets. Some stole to support their families and were sent to prison, leaving their children in slums or overcrowded streets to shine shoes, sell newspapers, or peddle matches to support themselves.

Charitable institutions overflowed with needy people. In 1853, a preacher who visited the almshouses in New York was moved by the problems that overpopulation had created. Charles Loring Brace founded the Children's Aid Society and began a program known as "placing out"—seeking new homes for disadvantaged children with farm families in other parts of the country. In 1854 the first group was loaded into a boxcar and sent west. Similarly, the New York Foundling Hospital, operated by the Sisters of Charity, began to relocate children abandoned at the hospital. The New England Home for Little Wanderers, The Salvation Army, and other organizations formed similar programs.

The Foundling Society typically placed infants and arranged homes for babies before they were put on the trains. Each baby was given a number that was sewed to its clothing. When the baby arrived at its destination, a person who had a card from the Foundling Society bearing a corresponding number would claim the baby. The Children's Aid Society usually sent children between the ages of five and twelve. CAS sent announcements to churches or community leaders, stating that the orphan train would arrive on a particular day. When the train stopped at the depot, the children were placed on the platform and selected by their new families. Often siblings were separated and never saw one another again. Adoptive families signed agreements for keeping the children, but due to the lack of regulation, periodic checks on the children's well-being were not always made.

Though each child's circumstance was unique, they shared some similarities. The sense that they never really belonged to anyone or any family was common. Most were never formally adopted. Others were treated as farm labor, never accepted by the family or even allowed to share family meals. Many children also experienced the stigma of being orphans. In those days, people felt that something was wrong with the children because no one wanted them.

About two hundred orphan train riders are living today. Even though they are not formally related, a "family reunion" takes place every year at the St. Francis Center in Little Falls, Minnesota. Sister Justina Bieganek, who boarded an orphan train from New York in 1913 wearing the number forty-one, organizes the gathering so that they might reminisce about their common bond.

At each reunion, an orphan tells his or her story, or a family member honors them by telling the story for them. My grandmother, Marjorie Peterson, rode the orphan train in November 1906. My mother, Betty Hengemuhle, volunteered to tell my grandmother's story at the 2002 gathering. Grandma had written her autobiography, but it remained private until her death in 1991. When Mom asked for my help, I decided no ordinary presentation would do justice to my grandmother's story. The only way to capture her special life was in a quilt. I surprised my mother with the gift of the quilt for her seventy-fifth birthday.

I struggled to find the perfect name for the quilt and suggested to my mom that perhaps a favorite song title would work. She quickly said, "The Green, Green Grass of Home." And that is what I put on her old handkerchief with tatting that is now the label on the back side of the quilt.

I used the quilt to tell my grandmother's heartwarming story at the orphan train rider reunion in August 2002. Since then I've told her story hundreds of times to audiences at all types of gatherings across the United States.

I've been quilting for more than thirty years and have made more than one hundred fifty quilts. I consider the quilt based on my grandmother's life to be my most memorable. My mother and I plan to donate "The Green, Green Grass of Home" and my grandmother's autobiography to a history museum some day so her story will live on and on.

My grandma would be proud to know that her story is living on. I wish that I had made the quilt sooner so that she could have seen it. However, I sewed an angel on the quilt and believe that each time her story is told, an angel will carry the message to her.

ಞ 1 ಬಃ

ANN, THIS IS YOUR MOM."
Betty began every phone call she made to her daughter, Ann, with that familiar statement. Ann always recognized her mother's quiet voice, but her mother still began every phone call with the same five words. The familiarity and sound of her mom's voice made Ann smile.

Betty's phone calls were always for something quick. Or so she intended. Betty didn't like to talk on the phone. She said it was a waste of time. There were many more productive things to do. Once the conversation started, however, it was like letting the cord loose on a tightly wound top. The conversation typically began with the matter at hand; however, it usually changed quickly to the status of a sewing project that she or Ann was working on, or a treasured find at a local garage sale, or news about one of the ol' neighbors on France Avenue, where Ann grew up in Robbinsdale, a Minneapolis suburb. "Hi, Mom. How are you today? What's up?"

"I had a phone call from Myrt this morning."

Betty's older sister, Myrt Nelson, lived in Long Prairie, a small town about one hundred twenty miles northwest of the Twin Cities of Minneapolis and St. Paul in Minnesota.

1

"How's Myrt? What's new in Long Prairie?" Ann sipped her coffee as she waited for her mom's reply.

"Well, I'm afraid she didn't have the best news. It's Grandma."

Ann placed her coffee cup on the table. "What's wrong? Is Grandma okay? Did she fall?"

Ann's grandmother, Marjorie Peterson, lived alone. She had lived in the same small, white house with dark-green trim on Todd Street as long as Ann could remember. Marjorie, ninety-three years old, had fallen a few years before while tying up a hydrangea bush in the front yard. Marjorie broke her pelvis when she took a quick, hard fall on the ground, but recovered well from the incident, despite her age. The family suggested that she give up her house and move to the sparkling new senior residence less than a block away where many of her friends lived. She could even have the same view from her apartment. Marjorie had no intention of leaving her quaint little house on Todd Street. A senior residence wasn't for her. End of subject.

"No she didn't fall, but she hasn't been feeling very well. Seems she got sick to her stomach last weekend, and she hasn't been able to shake it. When Grandma woke up this morning the pain in her stomach was so bad that she could barely get out of bed. She called Myrt."

There were seven children in the Peterson family. Myrt, Marjorie's second oldest daughter, lived about six blocks from her mother in Long Prairie, the town where she grew up. Shirley, the eldest, lived in Salt Lake City. Hazel and her husband, Eugene, owned a dairy farm on the outskirts of Long Prairie. Gerald, the oldest boy in the family, worked as a large crane operator in Lexington, Kentucky, where he lived with his wife Betty. Marv, the middle boy, lived almost in Marjorie's backyard. He was the proprietor of Long Prairie Lanes, the town bowling alley. Elly, the youngest, lived in Walnut Creek, a suburb of San Francisco.

Ann listened carefully. "Grandma told Mryt that she wanted to go to the doctor, so you know she isn't feeling well." That was all that Myrt needed to hear. She knew her mother's pain must have been severe because Marjorie never wanted to see a doctor unless there was a real need. "When Myrt arrived at Grandma's house, she helped her get dressed. She told Myrt that she had diarrhea and noticed some blood in her stool. Grandma was too weak and in too much pain to walk, so Myrt used Grandpa's old wheelchair to get her to the car."

Marjorie's husband, George, died December 29, 1983, a couple weeks after Marjorie and George celebrated their sixty-fourth wedding anniversary. George, a very tall man at least six feet, three inches, had very long legs in comparison to his short torso. He was confined to a wheelchair for about a year before he died because his knees were weak and unreliable, which made him very unstable when he walked.

"Where is Grandma now?" Ann asked her mother.

"The doctor admitted her to the hospital right away. She's pretty dehydrated. I don't know why she didn't tell someone before she got so sick. But you know Grandma. She doesn't want to trouble anyone."

Ann listened carefully as her mom described her mother. *Apple doesn't fall far from the tree*, Ann thought as her mom continued. Sounds just like something her mom would do. Never liked to put anyone out. "Are you and Dad going to Long Prairie?" Ann asked.

"The doctor's going to run some tests. Myrt will call me back this afternoon. I'll let you know what I hear. I need to make some more calls. I'll talk to you later."

Ann hung up the phone. She sat quietly and looked out the kitchen window. A bright yellow finch flew to the birdfeeder at the edge of the yard. Its companion was right behind. The small birds nibbled at the seed and hurriedly flew away.

Ann thought about the last time that she had seen her grandma. It was at a party for Marjorie's birthday in June when family and a few of Marjorie's friends gathered for cake and ice cream. Marjorie was at her best when there were people around. If they didn't come to see her, she would go to them. She was happiest when she was with a circle of family or friends.

The warm summer day dragged on as Ann waited with nervous anticipation for her mother's call. It was difficult to start on a project until she got word about the results of Grandma's tests. Ann finally heard from her mother late in the evening.

"Ann, this is your mom." Ann smiled at the familiar words.

"Did you hear from Myrt? Did they get the results of Grandma's tests?" Ann asked with concern.

"Yes. Myrt called from the hospital. Hazel and Marv were there, too. They met with the doctor."

"What did the doctor say? Is she going to be okay?"

"I'm sorry but the news isn't very good. I'm afraid that Grandma didn't get sick from something she ate. It's much more than that. The doctor found a mass in her abdomen. A surgeon could operate and try to remove the mass or do a biopsy, but she's much too weak." Ann listened carefully as her mother described the severity of her grandmother's condition. "They have her on an IV to keep her hydrated. She can't even keep water down. They're giving her medication for pain. Myrt said that she's sleeping now. Dad and I are going to Long Prairie early tomorrow morning. I'll call you from the hospital after we see Grandma."

"Have a safe trip and be sure to give me a call as soon as you know more. I'll be waiting for your call. Give my best to Grandma."

Ann tried to occupy herself with jobs around the house, but she couldn't let the thought of her ailing grandmother leave her mind. She fondly remembered family trips to Long Prairie when she was a child. Her family spent many, many weekends and special holidays at Grandma's house.

Marjorie's house was small. It had two bedrooms. The guest bedroom also served as Marjorie's sewing room. Ann's mom and dad always slept in the guest bedroom when they visited. Ann, and her older sister, Carol, slept on the living room floor under the cookoo clock that hung on the wall. Ann laughed to herself as she remembered the little wooden bird in that clock. It came out faithfully and chirped every hour on the hour all night long.

Family trips to Grandma's house in Long Prairie were always fun. There was so much to do, even if it meant just following her grandmother around and about town. Marjorie gave tirelessly of herself. She was always busy.

Marjorie served as president of the Long Prairie chapter of the Women's Relief Corps for twenty-two years. The corps honored the men and women who served the United States in war. She made sure that her chapter had a significant role in Long Prairie's celebrations for Memorial Day and the Fourth of July, Marjorie's favorite holidays. They sold red crepe paper poppies on street corners to raise funds for war veterans. They decorated veterans' graves at the cemetery. Most noteworthy, they were responsible for the annual Memorial Day event at the Long Prairie cemetery. Uniformed personnel from all branches of the service gathered in honor of the holiday. The color guard shot a twenty-one gun salute as a tribute to their fallen comrades. Marjorie always led the audience in the pledge of allegiance followed by the singing of the national anthem at the end of the program.

To Marjorie's disappointment, the national Women's Relief Corps disbanded in 1968 due to a lack of interest. She respected those who courageously served the country, doing whatever she could to show her appreciation. To her dismay, though, not everyone shared her untiring patriotism.

Marjorie was always involved in the grand ceremony of the community event for the Fourth of July. Ann smiled. She remembered the pride and sparkle in her grandmother's eyes when she carried the American flag down Main Street and throughout town for the Fourth of July parade. One time Marjorie called the Long Prairie radio station on the Fourth of July and told them that they should play more patriotic music and marches in honor of the holiday. Ann chuckled to herself. That was Grandma; she wasn't afraid to speak her mind.

Sometimes Marjorie called the *The Leader*, the local newspaper, when her family came to Long Prairie, even if it was just to spend the weekend. *The Leader* printed their names in the "WHAT'S HAPPENING" column in the paper, as though their visit was some kind of big event. Marjorie knew that it wasn't big news. She did it mostly for the excitement that it gave her grandchildren to read their names in print in the newspaper.

Betty and her husband, Hank, drove to Long Prairie at dawn the next morning. It was a two-hour drive from the Twin Cities. Hank and Betty arrived at Long Prairie Memorial Hospital about 8:00 a.m. The receptionist greeted them as they made their way up to the main desk inside the front doors of the hospital. "May I help you?" The young woman at the front desk greeted them with a friendly smile.

"My mother, Marjorie Peterson, is a patient here. Can you give me directions to her room?" Betty asked anxiously.

The young woman looked at the patient list that lay on the wooden desk in front of her. "Marjorie, Marjorie Peterson." She ran her finger on the list in front of her. "Oh, here she is. She's in room 135. Go down this hall," she motioned. "Take the first right. She's in the second room on the left."

Betty thanked the young woman. She and Hank walked quickly down the shiny tile hallway. It was eight years since they had been in the Long Prairie hospital. The last time was when Betty's father, George, was there. George's health had been declining steadily over the previous months. He had had a stroke while at home. They transported him to the hospital in an ambulance. He died less than twenty-four hours later at the age of ninety-five.

Betty and Hank arrived at room 135. They peered into the small, sterile room. Marjorie lay still in her bed. She was sleeping soundly. A nurse dressed in a bright blue smock was changing the plastic bag of clear liquid that was connected to Marjorie with an intravenous tube. Myrt and Marv sat in chairs on the opposite side of the room. The nurse completed her work and slipped quietly from the room.

"Betty, Hank, glad you're here. How was your trip?" Myrt and Marv greeted them as they entered the room.

"Mom didn't have a very good night last night," Marv whispered in a quiet voice. "She was in considerable pain. They gave her some more medication. She's been sleeping for quite a while."

Betty walked to her mother's bedside. Marjorie was sleeping soundly, a result of the meds. Betty smoothed the soft, white hospital blanket. As she gently tucked it snuggly around her mother's neck, she felt the warmth that came from her body. She looked so peaceful, so calm.

"Marv and I talked with Dr. Powers this morning," Myrt said quietly. "He said there really isn't anything that they can do for her without surgery; just keep her as comfortable as possible. She's too weak for surgery; she'd never make it." Myrt walked to Marjorie's bedside. "Hazel went home. She's helping Eugene with the chores. She called Shirley, Gerald, and Elly. They're all making arrangements to come home. Hazel'll know more about their travel plans when she comes back to the hospital."

Marjorie stirred in her bed. She coughed and opened her eyes. Betty gently rubbed the back of her hand on her mother's soft cheek. The usual rosy red color was no longer there. She looked pale. "Mom, Mom. It's Betty. I'm here." Marjorie turned her head slowly and opened her eyes. "Are you thirsty? Would you like a sip of water?"

Marjorie shook her head. "Who else is here, Betty? Is Hank with you?"

"Yes, Mom. Hank and I came from the Cities this morning. Myrt and Marv are here, too. Hazel went home to help Eugene with the chores. She'll be coming back in a little while."

Apologetically, Marjorie said, "I'm sorry to make you come all this way." Betty used a tissue to dab her mother's nose. "Did you talk with the doctor this morning?" Marjorie asked.

"Yes, Myrt and Marv talked with Dr. Powers." Betty wasn't quite sure what she was going to say next. Just then Reverend Lynn walked in the room.

"Mom, look who came to see you. It's Reverend Lynn." Betty extended her hand to Reverend Lynn. He took Betty's hand and then gave her a gentle hug.

Marjorie was an active member of the United Methodist Church of Long Prairie. She had joined the church in 1919, the year she and George were married. George hadn't often gone to church. He left that up to Marjorie. Anyone who attended a wedding or a funeral at the church usually found Marjorie in the kitchen or dining hall, preparing or serving the food for one of those occasions. She was a very active in the church's Ladies Aid Group. The group always charged her with making coffee.

Reverend Lynn leaned on the silver metal railing of Marjorie's hospital bed. He whispered in a gentle tone, "Marjorie, my dear friend, I'm sorry to see that you're not feeling well." Marjorie struggled to keep her eyes open. "I'm bringing you best wishes and many prayers from all your friends at church. They're all thinking about you and praying for you." Reverend Lynn placed his right hand gently on the white blanket that covered Marjorie. He bowed his head and said a short prayer.

Marjorie whispered a quiet, "Amen." in unison with her pastor and then closed her eyes and slipped off to sleep.

ॐ 2 ॐ

I T WAS A HOT DAY. The early afternoon temperature was eight-five degrees. The weather forecast was for even more heat and humidity. Leaves hung motionless on the trees. A breath of wind would help cut the humidity, but it never came.

Parked cars lined both sides of Todd Street. Marjorie's small and usually quiet house was filled with people. Strategically placed fans moved the warm air inside.

Marjorie and George lived in Long Prairie most of their married lives. They relocated to Portland, Oregon, in 1945 because they had heard that job opportunities were better in that part of the country. After job hunting, George found a job at the M&M Woodworking Company. Marjorie worked at Doernbecker Furniture Company in the factory. Later she took a job at Bamans Plastic Company where she assembled duck decoys.

George and Marjorie decided to move back to Long Prairie in 1958 because they wanted to live close to their family that was growing by leaps and bounds. Over the years their seven children had blessed them with twenty grandchildren, twenty-five great grandchildren and three great-great grandchildren. They longed to be with their family

At age fifty-six in Portland, Oregon.

regularly especially during the Christmas holiday season and at summer get-togethers such as family reunions and picnics.

George and Marjorie purchased a small white house with shake siding and dark green shutters at 227 Todd Street. Their children had moved out on their own, and the house was comfortable for George and Marjorie. It had two bedrooms—one for them and another that could be used as Marjorie's sewing room or a bedroom for an occasional overnight guest. The house was conveniently located a few blocks —an easy walk—from downtown Long Prairie. The large flat backyard was home to Marjorie's abundant vegetable and flower gardens. A one-car garage stood at the side of the house but was used mostly as a garden shed or occasionally for housing someone else's car.

The aroma of fresh-brewed coffee permeated the air in the cozy house. Marjorie's old coffee pot worked overtime on the kitchen counter, occupying the corner of the stained vinyl counter next to the old yellow metal bread box.

Everything in the house was exactly the way Marjorie had left it a few days earlier. As usual, the dining room table was covered with a lacy white tablecloth that she had crocheted. The dark wood of the old dining table peered through the designs she had crocheted and accented her lovely handwork. Marjorie loved a wide array of handcrafts. She especially enjoyed working on a craft project in the evening while she sat in her petite wooden rocker. Nat King Cole and Tennessee Ernie Ford, two of her favorite musical artists, serenaded her from phonograph records that she played over and over while she worked.

A bearded man in a green-and-black-plaid wool shirt bowed his head and folded his hands in prayer over a loaf of bread and Bible in the painting that hung above the dining table. The picture had hung there as long as anyone could remember. The table was crowded with plates that were overflowing with homemade cookies and pans of freshly baked bars. A few bouquets of brightly colored flowers were scattered about the room and a stack of unopened greeting cards peaked out of a brown wicker basket on Marjorie's small maple-colored wooden desk.

A bundle of envelopes—marked "bills to be paid"—were bound by a rubber binder, a date on each envelope noting when it was due to be paid.

Visitors came and went from the little house, most staying a short while, greeting the family, and expressing their condolences. Marjorie died on Saturday, August 24, 1991. She passed quietly during the night. She was in the hospital for only a few days before she succumbed to the illness that took her life. The medical staff lessened her pain, making her as comfortable as possible in her final days.

"Seems funny, Mom," Ann said to her mother as her eyes scanned the dining room and living room of Marjorie's house. "All these people at Grandma's house. This is just the way she liked it. She was at her best with a group of her friends or relatives. I almost expect to see her walk out of the kitchen. I can just picture her in an aqua-colored house dress and an embroidered gingham apron." Aqua was Marjorie's favorite color.

"Don't forget those funny little brown shoes that she always wore," Ann's older sister, Carol, added. Carol had arrived earlier in the day from Iowa City.

Marjorie had extremely large bunions on the sides of both of her feet. They were usually bursting through the sides of her well-worn brown shoes. The family tried to encourage Marjorie to have the bunions surgically removed, but she never would. Her feet must have caused her considerable pain, but she never complained. She persevered in her delightful way. Perhaps she thought that the surgery would have slowed her.

Visitors continued to come and go from the small house on Todd Street, some staying and visiting with the family. Others dropped off food to share or placed a greeting card in the wicker basket on the table next to Marjorie's small wooden rocker. Despite efforts to move the air with fans, the house was extremely warm, the air thick with humidity.

"It's way too hot and humid in this house for me. I need to get some air. Maybe I can catch a breeze outside. Would you like to join me, Mom?" Ann asked. "I'm going outside for a few minutes."

"I think I will, too, before I wilt."

Ann and her mom squeezed their way through the small kitchen, and they walked down a few steps and into the breezeway. Marjorie's muddy garden shoes waited in the corner near the door. The shoes were very worn and shaped for Marjorie's decrepit-looking feet. The concrete slab outside the screen door was cracked and crumbling. Ann held the screen door open for her mom. "Watch your step, Mom. I didn't realize that this slab was so uneven," Ann said as she looked at the broken concrete. "How did Grandma walk out here without falling on her face, especially with her bad feet?"

"Good question," Betty said as she walked gingerly to the garden path." A narrow concrete path sloped gently to a small grassy backyard. Faded blue morning glories, wilted from the heat of the day, climbed the white wooden trellis on the side of the garage. Yellow, red, and pink gladiolas stood in formation at the back of the garage. Masses of red and purple petunias overflowed from black cast-iron pots.

Ann and Betty paused to take in the beautiful colors of Marjorie's flower garden. "She sure loved her flowers, didn't she?" Ann thought for a moment. "Mom, do you remember the time when Grandma brought Grandpa out to the garden when he was in his wheelchair?" Ann smiled as she recalled the incident.

Betty chuckled softly. "I was just thinking the same thing."

George had been confined to a wheelchair the last year of his life. Often, on a nice day, Marjorie had wheeled George into the backyard, so that he could soak in the warmth of the sun and get some fresh air. He sat in the chair near the corner of the garage with a good view of Marjorie as she worked in the garden. One day when she wheeled George outside, she let go of the wheelchair and then turned to pull the screen door shut. Inadvertently, she neglected to lock the wheels on George's chair.

He started to roll freely down the uneven concrete path, slowly at first and then quickly gaining speed. He thought that Marjorie was pushing the chair. He yelled, "Ma, don't you think you're going a little fast. Ma, slow down. You're going too fast."

Marjorie with her rhododendrons.

Marjorie realized that George's chair was on the loose when he began to yell. She chased after him but wasn't nearly swift enough to catch the free-wheeling chair. The chair hit a step at the edge of the garden and stopped suddenly, which caused George to catapult freely from the chair. He landed with a thud in the first row of peas. Fortunately, he wasn't injured.

"Sure lucky that Grandpa wasn't hurt."

"Isn't that the truth? Betty said with a sigh of relief. "I think he was almost ninety-five years old when it happened. Funny he didn't break into a million pieces. It's one of those incidents that are really scary at the time. Fortunately, the incident had a happy ending, and we can laugh today because he wasn't hurt."

A light breeze cooled the heavy summer air briefly. Ann put her face into the air to catch it. "Feels a bit cooler out here, doesn't it? It was getting way too warm in the house for me."

Ann and Betty continued down the path that divided the garden. They passed rows of peas, beans, lettuce, cabbage, and potatoes on one side with raspberries, strawberries, radishes, and carrots on the other. "Look at this garden! She sure had a green thumb." Ann stopped and picked a bright red raspberry and popped it into her mouth. "I wish I would've inherited her green thumb and gardening skill."

"I wonder how many hundreds of pints of berries she froze through the years," Betty questioned. "Oh, how delicious they tasted in a bowl of sweet cream in the middle of January."

"I think my favorite was leaf lettuce salad," Ann replied. "I don't know what she put in the creamy dressing that she made, but I think I could eat the whole bowl of salad on my own."

Ann and Betty paused at the end of the garden. The Long Prairie high school building cast a shadow on the garden from across the street.

"Do you remember when she used to sell her vegetables to the Long Prairie High School for their hot lunch program?" Marjorie was an enterprising woman. Frequently she loaded produce from her garden into her wheelbarrow, wheeled it across the street, and sold it to the high school. "Her cabbages were so huge that sometimes three or four cabbages would fill the deep wheelbarrow. Any idea how many years she sold her vegetables to the high school?"

Betty laughed quietly and shook her head. "Oh, it's really hard to say. I'm sure scores of Long Prairie students grew up eating her produce." Ann and Betty turned and started to walk back to the house. "I'm sure you could find the answer to that question in Grandma's diaries. You know she wrote everything down." Marjorie had kept a daily diary for over forty years. She journaled everything from the birth of grandchildren to how much she was paid for a wheelbarrow of vegetables. A complete family history was contained in the pages of her diaries.

"Do you have any idea where Grandma kept her diaries?" Ann questioned.

"Oh, I suppose they're in the house somewhere. She kept everything so organized. She even wrote the date she bought a bag of sugar on the outside of the bag."

"Grandma gave me a blank diary one year for a Christmas gift. It had a red cover with a gold lock. She encouraged me to write. I remember asking her about when she wrote in her journal. She told me that every day after she made her bed, she would sit on the end of it and make the entry from the previous day. What a wonderful written treasure we have in her writing. Is it okay if I snoop around this evening? I'd really like to read what she wrote."

"Sure, if you like. You'll probably find everything from the date she bought her first washing machine and what she paid for it to what she bought each of the grandkids for Christmas over that past forty years. She kept track of everything."

Ann and Betty made their way up the garden path and into the house. The afternoon was drawing to a close and evening approaching. Most of the visitors had left. Myrt and Hazel were in the tiny kitchen warming casseroles and taking aluminum foil covers off bowls of gelatin salads and desserts. Shirley dipped soiled coffee cups into soapy water in the kitchen sink and then rinsed them in a steady stream of warm water. "Have you ever seen so much food?" Myrt said to Hazel, as Betty and Ann made their way through the back door and into the kitchen.

"Didn't we just finish eating lunch? It can't be time to eat again, can it?" Ann asked as she put her hand to her stomach.

"Someone has to eat all this food; otherwise I don't know what we're going to do with it. Maybe we can take some of it to the church for the luncheon after the funeral tomorrow." Myrt lifted the aluminum foil from another glass bowl to see what it contained. Betty stopped in the kitchen to help Myrt and Hazel. Ann slid past them. She walked through the dining room and into the guest bedroom. The room was just the way that Marjorie had left it. The bed was covered with a white chenille spread, and two round pillows that Marjorie had crocheted with bright-colored yarn lay against the pillows on the bed. Carefully, Ann lifted the corner of the spread at the top edge of the bed and peaked at the hand-embroidered pillowcases with pink flowers and yellow butterflies. Light-pink variegated crocheted lace finished the edges of the cases. Just as she thought. Anyone who ever slept at Marjorie's house always slept on a hand-embroidered pillowcase with crotched lace on the edge. Ann tucked the spread neatly in place and smoothed it with her hand.

Across the small room, under the window was Marjorie's sewing machine. The brown wood case was closed. A doilie with tatted lace that Marjorie had made covered the top of the case. Ann fingered the lacey white doilie. Marjorie had given her one just like it for Christmas one year.

Marjorie's hands had never been idle. She loved all sorts of handwork. There were usually several copies of *Workbasket Magazine*, a crafter's periodical, on her coffee table. She was always excited to show her most recent project. Each of her twenty grandchildren was the proud owner of one of Marjorie's beautiful crotched afghans.

Ann rubbed her hand on the worn front edge of the sewing machine case. Marjorie loved to sew. She had sewn everything from window curtains to quilts and sat for hours at her sewing machine. The wood at the front of the sewing cabinet was worn from where she rested her arms. In 1969, after the Women's Relief Corps disbanded, Marjorie started sewing lap quilts. She donated them to the veterans' home. At last count, she had made 359 of them.

Marjorie was a utilitarian quilter, in the finest sense of the word. She was always scrounging and looking for scraps of fabric for the patchwork on the front of the quilt, batting to make it warm or fabric for the quilt backing. She never declined a donation of fabric. Most of her quilts were tied with brightly colored yarn. Ann smiled and thought of her grandma's quilts. They were real patchwork quilts. She made the most of every square inch of fabric that she had on hand. I'm sure she never set foot on the floor of one of the lovely quilt shops around today with bolts and bolts of coordinated fabrics, Ann thought.

On the wall above the sewing machine was a framed award that Marjorie won. Ann stopped to read it: "Marjorie M. Peterson, Long Prairie, Minnesota – Todd County Outstanding Senior Citizen – 1986." Governor Rudy Perpich's signature and seal of the State of Minnesota were at the bottom. Marjorie had been recognized by the state as her county's outstanding senior citizen at the age of eighty-eight. She went to the Minnesota State Fair and proudly received her award from the governor. It was a very proud day for Marjorie's family, her county, and the entire State of Minnesota.

A large cupboard filled the wall to the left of Marjorie's sewing machine. The cupboard stretched from the floor nearly to the ceiling and was covered by two large wooden doors. Ann pulled gently on the wooden button-style knob. The door didn't open. The wood was swollen from the humidity, a typical result of humid Minnesota summer weather. Ann pulled again. This time the door opened with a jolt. She peered inside at the neatly stacked closet shelves. Each cardboard box was labeled with its contents on the outside. A dozen or more photograph albums stood straight, side by side on one shelf. Two shoeboxes, stacked on top of each other and labeled "Diaries," held the albums in place like a bookend.

Grandma and Rudy Perpich at the State Fair, 1986.

Ann reached into the cupboard and pulled the top shoebox from the shelf. The photograph albums leaned to the left. Slowly, Ann lifted the corner of the box lid. Quickly, she put the cover back down. She was eager to see the contents of the box; however, she felt like she was violating her grandmother's privacy. Ann paused with the dark-brown shoe box in her hands and then walked to Marjorie's sewing machine. She pulled the chair out from behind the cabinet and sat down, resting the box on her lap. She wanted to look at the diaries. She really wanted to read them. What would Grandma think if she knew she was snooping through her cupboards, not to mention that she was about to read her private diaries? But, were they really her private diaries now? She wouldn't have written in them if she didn't want them to be read some day, would she? Ann stared at the top of the dark-brown box. Slowly, she lifted the cover from the box and set it on top of the sewing machine cabinet. The inside of the box smelled old. It contained several small books, each one a different size and color. Some had clasps with locks on the outside, others were open books.

Ann removed the first diary from the box. The book had a black cover with gold-embossed writing that said, "My Diary." Marjorie had added a label that said "1955." Ann had been born in 1952 and was three years old at the time that this diary had been started. She didn't open the diary or read any part of it; rather she looked at the next book. It was labeled "1954." She dug to the bottom of the box. The book she removed was labeled "1949." That was the year that Ann's mother and father had been married. She wondered if she might find the details of her parents' wedding day inside.

Ann didn't read the diaries. Not yet. Instead, she went back to the cupboard and removed the second shoebox of diaries from the shelf. The weight of the leaning photo albums made them fall and lie flat on the shelf. Ann lifted them and pushed them back in place. They were only going to fall again, unless she found something with some weight to support them. She held the albums in place with her right hand while she glanced in the cupboard. She found a box labeled "6-inch polyester quilt squares." She pushed it in place against the photo albums. Just then she noticed the first book in the row of albums. It was significantly smaller than the rest. It was about the size of a secretary's shorthand tablet. The front and back covers were made from gray cardboard, similar to the back of a writing tablet. It wasn't a photograph album, like the other books.

Ann removed the small book from the shelf. Several sheets of paper filled the inside. Two holes were punched at the edge of the little gray-covered book. It was tied together with a narrow blue-and-white striped cording. On the cover, in Marjorie's handwriting it said, "My Autobiography, My Life – Marjorie Peterson."

"Oh, my gosh. I don't believe it," Ann gasped. "Grandma wrote her life story, " Ann whispered quietly to herself. She continued to stare at the front cover. She wondered if anyone else had ever seen this book. Carefully, she opened the front cover. Immediately she recognized her grandmother's handwriting on the first page. A folded sheet of paper lay inside the front cover.

Ann knew that her grandmother could write, and write well. She had written her letters all the time. Many she still had. She had no idea that her grandmother had written her life story.

Ann slowly made her way to the chair at Marjorie's sewing machine. She sat down and began to read. "My Life" was the simple sentence on the first line. "My birthday was May 17, 1898. I changed it to June 13, 1898."

"What?" Ann said out loud. "Grandma changed her birth date? You're kidding? Why?" Suddenly, Ann looked around. There was no one else in the room. The shock and amazement of what she read made her talk out loud to herself. The family had always celebrated June 13 as her grandmother's birthday. "Since when was she born on May 17? Does everyone else know this? Is this news only to me?"

Ann continued to read. "As I have been told, I was adopted by Philip and Josephine Sutton from a church home in St. Paul, Minnesota, the year of 1898. My name was Mary Sutton. They lived at Owatonna, Minnesota, as I can remember when I was about five years old. We lived in the country which was called Spring Road, Owatonna. They also had an older adopted son by the name of Willie Olmstead. He got in bad with two other boys named the Nelson brothers. They robbed and murdered a saloonkeeper. They were put in Owatonna jail, then went to Stillwater prison. Willie was about twenty years old."

Ann couldn't believe what she was reading. Had anyone else in the family read Grandma's autobiography? Did anyone even know that she had written her life story?

The family was still gathered in the living room a few feet from where Ann sat reading her grandmother's autobiography. She could hear the family sharing stories. The tone went from somber conversation to loud waves of laughter as someone shared a funny story of the past. Ann joined the family in the living room. She carried her grandmother's autobiography.

"Did you finally decide to come out and join us, Ann, and are you going to stand there the rest of the evening? How about a plate of food? Maybe you can do your part to help us eat up some of this food. Why don't you grab a plate?" Betty pointed at the dining room table that was overflowing with food. Every kind of casserole and gelatin dessert was represented. Rows of nine-by-thirteen-inch metal pans filled with desserts crowded a separate table. It looked like a scene from a church dinner at Lake Wobegon in Garrison Keilor's *Prairie Home Companion*.

"Did anyone here know that Grandma wrote her life story?" Ann looked around the room. "I found it in the cupboard in Grandma's sewing room. It was with all her photo albums."

Everyone in the room started to talk at once.

"I'm not surprised that Grandma would write her life story. You know she wrote in a diary almost every day for over forty years, didn't you?" Shirley said.

"I gave her blank diaries as Christmas gifts many years." Myrt added.

"I did, too," Hazel chimed in. "I knew she wrote in them, but I never read them."

"I found a shoebox with diaries from the 1940s and 1950s in the cupboard. Then I found another box of diaries. I was going to look at that box when I found her autobiography next to her photo albums." Ann held up the cardboard-covered book tied with cording. "I only read the first couple pages. I can't believe what she wrote. Did anyone here know that Grandma's real birthday was May 17 not June 13? She changed it to June 13. That's what she says anyway." No one made a comment. An eerie silence filled the room. "That's what it says right here on the front page." Ann read her grandmother's writing. "My birthday was May 17, 1898. I changed it to June 13, 1898."

Suddenly, everyone started talking at once. Relatives and friends guessed at what would make someone change her birthday. Ann sat on a small footstool at the edge of the room and listened. Exchanges of conversation changed quickly from Marjorie's birth date to stories about the past.

Ann opened Marjorie's autobiography. A small piece of paper fell to the floor. She unfolded it. She read to herself a poem that Marjorie had copied.

One Little Rose

I'd rather have one little rose
from the garden of a friend,
Than to have the choicest flowers
when my stay on earth must end.
I'd rather have the kindest words
which may now be said of me,
Than to be flattered when I'm gone
and my life has ceased to be.

I'd rather have a loving smile
from friends I know are true,
Than tears shed 'round my casket
when I've bade this world adieu.
Bring me all your flowers today
whether pink or white or red.
I'd rather have one blossom now
than a truckload when I'm dead.

At the bottom of the poem Marjorie had written, "I read this poem to a group at the Long Prairie Nursing Home one Sunday at a service we had there. It fits me just swell." She signed the bottom "Mom Peterson." How appropriate for today.

Family and friends continued to talk in the crowded living room. Ann walked back to the guest bedroom. She sat on the edge of the bed and continued to read the handwritten pages of the small gray cardboard-covered book. She read her grandmother's life story.

ঙ 3 ൠ

Josie, we have to hurry," Philip said. "The train to St. Paul's going to leave soon, and we can't be late. Are you sure that Minnie's expecting us? Does she know that we need to spend the night with her? We can't possibly return home from St. Paul before dark today."

Philip's older sister, Minnie, and her husband, Arthur Leake, lived in St. Paul, Minnesota. Arthur worked at a bank in the heart of the busy city. The train ride from Owatonna, a small town in southeastern Minnesota, to St. Paul, the state's capital, was at least two hours. "Yes, Philip, Minnie knows we're coming. I'm almost ready. I want to be sure that everything's buttoned up at home before we leave. I'm a bundle of nerves. I'm so excited about picking up our new baby girl, but I'm nervous about leaving the house without knowing Willie's whereabouts."

Philip went outside and boarded the wagon. He looked over his shoulder and gazed at the small white farm house with red trim. Adding a baby to their family would be a dramatic change, but he was looking forward to it. He and Josie had longed to have children for so long; he couldn't believe that their dream was going to come true in a few hours.

The plank flooring creaked as Josie moved nervously in the kitchen. She opened the door to the backyard and saw Philip who was

25

eagerly waiting for her in the wagon. Josie took a fleeting look into the tiny kitchen and then pulled the door closed tightly behind her. She ran to join Philip in the wagon.

Philip and Josie Sutton lived on a farm in the country, a few miles west of Owatonna, Minnesota, on Spring Road. Owatonna, a town of about fifty-five hundred people and predominantly a farming community, was set quietly into the rolling countryside of southern Minnesota.

Philip and Josie had grown up on adjacent farms. They had attended the same country school and were sweethearts from the first day that they had met. They were married soon after their high school graduation in May 1894. Philip's father gave them a parcel of his farm land as a wedding gift, and their families helped them build a house and barn on the property. They grew mostly corn and hay on the land while Josie tended a large vegetable garden that helped with their living. They also had a couple of dairy cows and several chickens.

Philip and Josie loved children and wanted to raise a large family. But about a year after they were married, Josie still wasn't pregnant despite their efforts. One day, Josie went to see a doctor in Owatonna and learned that she would never be able to conceive a child. Although Philip and Josie were very disappointed, they didn't want the doctor's news to discourage them from their dream of raising a family. Early in the spring of 1895 they decided to visit the State School Orphanage located outside Owatonna. People in town talked about the orphanage, but Philip and Josie didn't know much more than what they had heard.

The Minnesota State Public School for Dependent and Neglected Children had opened in December 1886, with three children. It was the brainchild of Hastings Hart. Boxcars of orphaned children had moved through the Midwest from overflowing orphanages in New York City and other overpopulated areas on the East Coast of the United States. These children, as well as locally orphaned and displaced children, needed homes. The goal of the State School Orphanage, as it came to be known, was to move the orphans into homes via adoption.

An orphanage official escorted Philip and Josie on a tour of the school property. He told the couple about the numerous orphaned or abandoned children needing good homes. Philip and Josie were saddened by the number of children they saw without homes. Most of the children were about five years old and older, into their early teens. The only babies at the orphanage at that time were one-month old twin girls. Josie didn't think that she wanted to start their family with two small babies. One baby would be plenty for her to handle, especially with the help she gave Philip with the crops and animals on their farm. Still she wouldn't think of adopting one of the twins without the other. Hopefully, the orphanage could find a home for them both so they could stay together.

The school official suggested to Philip and Josie that they consider adopting a teenage boy. The orphanage had several strong, young boys looking for homes. Surely one of them would like to go home with them. A strong, young boy could be a huge asset to Philip on the farm. After all, it was close to time to plant the crops.

The school official reviewed his register of available children. "Here's a fifteen-year-old boy named Willie—Willie Olmstead. He was born to a German mother and father in New York City. His father was killed while working at a company that printed newspapers. Willie's mother left him at an orphanage in New York City after she became very ill and couldn't care for him any longer. "Would you like to meet Willie? I can ask someone to bring him here so you can meet him."

Philip and Josie looked tentatively at each other. "What do you think, Philip? I was really hoping to adopt a much younger child, but a young man would be a big help to you on the farm."

Philip looked into Josie's bright green eyes as he patted her tightly clasped hands that lay on her lap. Philip shrugged his shoulders. With trepidation he asked Josie, "What do you think? Do you think that we should meet this young man?" Josie smiled faintly at Philip and nodded her head. "Yes, sir," Philip addressed the school official, "we'd like to meet this young man. You said his name is Willie? Is that right?"

"Yes, Willie Olmsted. Please excuse me while I ask someone to bring Willie here." The school official left the room, and Philip and Josie were grateful for the time to talk privately. Several minutes later, the school official returned with a tall, lanky young man whose curly dark hair was trimmed neatly above his ears. Gray-tweed wool trousers touched the tops of his worn boots. His long-sleeved blue-plaid shirt was buttoned neatly at his neck, but the tails stuck out at the waist of his trousers. He quickly tucked the shirt into his pants and then stood still, shyly lowering his head. He glanced upward with his sad-looking brown eyes when the school official spoke. "Mr. and Mrs. Sutton, I'd like you to meet Willie Olmstead." Willie stood quietly at the man's side.

Philip extended his hand to Willie. "Nice to meet you, Willie. I'm Philip Sutton. This is my wife, Josie." Willie shook Philip's hand. He nodded his head and smiled at Josie. "We live on a small farm not too far from here. We'd like to have you come to live with us. Would you like to come home with us?"

The orphanage where Willie had lived in New York City was big and overflowing with abandoned and orphaned children. He disliked the rules and structure there and one day had decided to try living on his own. He lived on the streets, selling matches on the corner or sometimes newspapers in order to support himself. Sometimes he stole just to be able to get one meal during the day. Often he slept out in the cold, under a staircase or in the doorway of a building. Hungry and cold and unable to support himself, Willie returned to the orphanage. It wasn't his first choice, but at least he would have a roof over his head and was guaranteed one hot meal every day. A couple of days after Willie returned to the orphanage, the only real home that he had, a matron there told Willie that he and some other children had been selected to go on a train to a new home. The train was destined for the Midwestern states of the United States where there were numerous farms and open country. Farm families in the Midwest were looking for children to take into their homes. Willie had never seen a farm and didn't have any idea what life on a farm might be like, but he thought he would give it a try. It had to be better than trying to survive on the dangerous, rat-infested streets of New York City.

When the train arrived at the depot in a small town outside Owatonna, Willie and the other children from the orphanage were led off the train to the depot platform. The matron directed the orphans to stand straight and tall. She brushed their tattered, wrinkled clothing, straightened their caps, and tried to make them as presentable and attractive as possible to the viewing audience.

People from the community, mostly farm families, gathered at the train depot. They looked quizzically at the homeless and pathetic children. It was simple. Pick a child from the train depot platform and take him or her home. It was that easy. Some of the children, eager to be selected, sang a song or performed a dance. They tried desperately to draw the audience's attention to themselves. Some orphans, traveling with brothers and sisters, clung tightly to their siblings, hoping that they would be selected by the same family, or at least within the same community, so their family wouldn't be broken up.

Harry and Alice Olson had walked up to Willie and looked him up and down. Mr. Olson planted his strong hands firmly on Willie's shoulders, turned him around and looked at him from the backside. In a thick, Swedish accent Mr. Olson asked Willie if he had ever lived on a farm.

"No, sir," Willie said.

Mr. Olson squeezed Willie's upper arm. "Feels like you have a bit of muscle, son. You'll get more from working on the farm." Mr. Olson pulled down on Willie's chin, opening Willie's mouth and peering inside. "Looks like you got good teeth. None missing anyway." Mr. Olson put his large, weathered-looking hands on Willie's shoulders. He looked Willie square in his eyes. "Boy, you won't give me and the wife any trouble now, will you?"

"No, sir!" Willie said with certainty.

Harry and Alice Olson had immigrated to the United States in 1885. They settled in Minnesota because the geography and climate were similar to Sweden, their homeland. The Olsons owned a dairy farm and also raised corn and hay. At first Willie liked living with the Olsons. They were older people, and their five children, all boys, were all grown and had moved away. The Olsons needed an extra hand on the farm. Willie worked hard for the Olsons at the beginning, but unfortunately he wasn't able to adapt to the culture of country living. He liked the wide open spaces of the country but missed the hustle and bustle of the city. He rarely saw anyone while out in the country. He was lonely and wanted some excitement in his life. Willie ran away. He traveled to Owatonna—not nearly as large or vibrant a city as New York City, but at least more exciting than the country. One day the owner of the Owatonna Mercantile caught Willie stealing merchandise from his store. He contacted the sheriff, who returned Willie to the Olsons. Willie ran away from home again and again. The last time the sheriff brought Willie home after he was caught stealing, the Olsons told the sheriff that they couldn't break him of his evil ways and asked the sheriff to take Willie to the State School Orphanage outside Owatonna. At a minimum, Willie would have a roof over his head and a warm meal, and perhaps the structure of the orphanage would help reform him.

"Willie," Philip said as he glanced at Josie from the corner of his eye, "we'd like you to come home with us. We don't have any children. We live on a small farm. We don't have a lot, but we'd like you to be a part of our family."

Willie looked quizzically at Philip. He wondered why the Suttons would want to adopt an orphan his age. *They're probably just like the Olsons,* Willie thought, *looking for someone to work on the farm.* Farm life didn't particularly appeal to Willie; he knew that from past experience. Going with the Suttons, however, could be the ticket that he was looking for to leave the orphanage.

"Yes, sir, I'd like to go home with you. Be part of your family," Willie answered with confidence.

Philip put his hand on Willie's shoulder. "Looks like we've got a deal, young man."

The orphanage official asked Philip and Josie to sign some paperwork while Willie went to another building to collect his things. Willie returned with a small brown satchel that he carried over his shoulder.

"Looks like you're all ready, Willie. The wagon's parked behind the building. I think we're all done here. Let's go to your new home."

Willie settled in quickly with Philip and Josie. Soon, however, Philip and Josie learned that Willie was skipping school and was frequently spending his days in town rather than in school. While in town, Willie met LeRoy and Virgil Nelson, brothers who were a few years older than Willie. They quickly became friends. Eventually, Willie was staying in town more than he was with Philip and Josie. He returned to the Suttons only when he needed a meal or a bed to sleep in. Although they had never met the boys, Philip and Josie knew LeRoy and Virgil Nelson were rough characters who had a poor reputation in town. They frequented the saloon and were always getting in to trouble of some sort. Philip and Josie weren't happy about the friendship that Willie had formed with the Nelson brothers.

After five years of marriage, Philip and Josie still wanted to have children. They knew that they would have to adopt because they couldn't conceive a child of their own. Philip and Josie were disheartened with their adoption experience at the State School Orphanage and decided not to adopt another child from that facility, not even an infant. They learned from Philip's sister, Minnie, that a church home in St. Paul was looking for families to adopt orphaned and abandoned babies. Philip and Josie immediately corresponded with the church home. Within a couple weeks, they received a letter informing them that they had been selected to adopt a two-month-old baby girl who had been abandoned at the church home.

๑ 4 ๘

JOSIE HANDED PHILIP A SMALL PACKAGE and then climbed into the wagon. She sat close to Philip on the wooden wagon seat. "I wish Willie would have come home to take us to the train. He said he would. He knew that we were planning to leave for a couple days." Irritated and anxious, Josie asked, "Where *is* he anyway?"

"We can't worry about that now or we'll be late to meet the train. We'll take the buggy to town and leave it. George at the livery can take care of the horse until we come home on Friday," Philip said.

Josie held a small package of articles for their new baby on her lap. She was so excited about the prospect of their new baby girl that she had hardly slept a wink all night. She thought about what it would feel like finally to hold the tiny baby in her arms. They had waited a long time for this extraordinary day.

They arrived at the depot just minutes before the train was scheduled to depart. Philip and Josie boarded the train and collapsed into their seats. Within moments the whistle blew, and the train moved forward with a jerk. They both breathed a heavy sigh of relief. How unfortunate it would have been to miss the train to pick up their new baby daughter. The train started slowly and gradually picked up speed as it traveled through town. "Look Josie," Philip called out with surprise as he pointed out the train window. "Look, there's Willie!" he exclaimed. "No wonder he didn't come home to drive us to the depot. He's with those Nelson brothers, and it looks like they've been drinking again." Willie and the Nelson brothers were laughing and stumbling about. Sadly, they were heading back towards the saloon.

THE TRAIN ARRIVED IN ST. PAUL AS SCHEDULED. It was a beautiful July day —bright sunshine and a gentle breeze—a picture-perfect day for Philip and Josie to pick up their baby. It seemed inconceivable that they were finally going to start the family that they had longed to have for so many years.

Philip and Josie traveled to the church home where the nuns had been caring for their baby daughter since she was abandoned a couple months before. Josie held tightly to Philip's arm as they made their way up the steps to the entry of the cold-looking, formidable, gray-stone building. "I hope they like us," Josie said.

"Oh, Josie, what's not to like about you. You'll be a wonderful mother for our new baby." Josie appreciated Philip's kind comments but wondered if he was right. Look at Willie. He was always getting into some sort of trouble or other. She hadn't done a very good job raising him. Philip knew exactly what Josie was thinking. "This is different, Josie. We're going to have a fresh start with a baby that we can call our own." Philip lifted the cast-iron door knocker and let it fall against the metal plate on the large wooden door. A slender lady, dressed in a long black dress opened the door. "May I help you?" she said in a whisper-quiet voice.

"Yes, I'm Philip Sutton and this is my wife, Josie. We're here to adopt a baby girl that you've been caring for."

"Oh, yes, Mr. and Mrs. Sutton, we've been expecting you. Please come in. I'm Sister Margaret. I'll find Sister Irene for you." Sister Margaret guided Philip and Josie into the front room of the convent.

She glided gracefully in her long, black habit that was gathered loosely at her waist with a beaded belt that looked like a giant rosary. A wooden cross hung at the end of the belt. Sister Margaret motioned for Philip and Josie to sit in upholstered straight-back chairs on the far side of a large wooden desk. "You must be tired and thirsty from your train ride. Let me get you some water to drink."

Sister Margaret left the room and returned with two glasses on a tray and a large pitcher of cold water. Sister Irene followed her into the room. Philip and Josie stood up as the elderly nun entered. Philip tucked his cap under his arm.

"Hello, I'm Sister Irene."

Philip held out his hand. "Sister Irene. Pleased to meet you, ma'am. I'm Philip Sutton, and this is my wife, Josie. We've been looking forward to coming here for several weeks."

Sister Irene sat on the opposite side of the large desk. She folded her aged hands and laid them on a stack of papers in front of her.

"You look like a very nice couple, Mr. and Mrs. Sutton. We received your adoption paperwork in the mail, and everything appears to be in order. I have just one more document for you to sign." She slid a piece of paper across the desk to Philip and showed him where to sign. Josie watched as Philip signed his name at the bottom of the paper. Sister Irene took the piece of paper from Philip and placed it in the stack. "I'll bring the baby to you."

Nervously, Josie spoke, "Sister Irene, can you tell me anything about our baby's mother?" Josie's voice cracked. "Did you know her? Did you meet her?"

Sister Irene replied very firmly, "Yes, I did meet her. We're not allowed, however, to tell you anything about the mother. I'll get the baby now."

Sister Irene turned and walked from the dimly lit room. Her long black habit flowed after her. Josie was even more anxious. She hoped that she hadn't asked a question that would put their adoption in jeopardy. A large clock on the wall ticked loudly and broke the silence of the quiet room. It seemed like hours, but within moments Sister Irene returned with a small pink bundle in her arms. Philip and Josie jumped to their feet. Carefully, Sister Irene passed the tiny baby into Josie's outstretched arms.

PHILIP AND JOSIE STEPPED CAREFULLY DOWN the gray-stone steps of the church home and onto the sidewalk. It had been a very long day, beginning with their train ride from Owatonna to St. Paul. Now they needed to make their way to Minnie and Arthur's house, where they would spend the night before they returned to Owatonna the following day. Josie carried the tiny bundle very close to her chest. Curious, she lifted the soft blanket and peeked at the tiny baby inside. She kissed her gently on the forehead. She could feel the baby's warm breath on her face. She couldn't believe that this baby was really theirs. It was true.

Philip carried their travel bag and a second, small bag that the nuns at the church home had given them. The bag contained milk in a bottle that was wrapped tightly in a cloth. It should stay warm enough for the baby until they arrived at his sister's house.

Philip hired a driver at a livery to take them to Minnie and Arthur's house. The walk was more than they could make, especially while carrying luggage and their new baby. Philip boarded the wagon, and the driver helped Josie into the wagon after she gingerly handed Philip the baby. The driver listened carefully to the street address that Philip gave him and then boarded the wagon. With a quick snap of the reins, the horses started walking, and the buggy jerked forward. The driver looked at Josie and the precious bundle that she carried. "That looks like a very tiny baby that you have, ma'am. How old is she?"

"She's two months old," Josie said in a whisper so she wouldn't wake the baby. "We just adopted her from the church home. Hard to believe that someone could give up this beautiful baby. We're going to stay with our family in St. Paul tonight. Tomorrow we'll take the train to our home in Owatonna." Josie couldn't take her eyes off their new daughter who started to stir and whimper softly. The baby moved her lips and struggled to open her tiny eyes. "Philip, would you please give me the bottle of milk. The baby's starting to fuss. I think she's hungry. I don't want her to cry. I want her to be at her best when she meets her new aunt and uncle for the first time." Josie unwrapped the warm bottle and put it to the baby's lips. She immediately began to inhale the contents. Even though she was a tiny baby she had a very hardy appetite.

The buggy traveled down a quiet street, just a few blocks from the busy city. Large brick houses lined both sides of the street while mature trees draped their branches over the roadway like a canopy. Each house had a walkway from the street to the front door. It had been a couple of years since Philip and Josie had visited Minnie and Arthur at their house. The driver pulled up in front of a red-brick house with white trim and shutters on the windows. It was a beautiful, stately house only six blocks from downtown St. Paul where Arthur worked. Minnie, a tall, willowy woman, was at the front of the house sweeping the porch with a broom. She looked up when the buggy stopped in front of the house. Immediately, she dropped the broom and walked quickly toward the street. She took off her apron while she walked.

"Oh, I'm so excited that you're here," Minnie said as she reached her arms out and gave Josie and the baby a hug. "It's been so long since we've seen you. We've missed you so much." Minnie pulled the blanket away from the baby's face. "Oh, my. Isn't she wonderful?" Minnie exclaimed. "It's been a long time since I've seen a newborn baby. Have I forgotten how small a new baby is, or is she a tiny little one?"

Josie looked down at the precious bundle in her arms. "I don't think you've forgotten the size of newborn, Minnie. She's a small baby. I'm sure it won't be long, and she'll grow like a weed."

Philip picked up their travel bag and the package that the nuns at the convent had given them. He paid the driver and the buggy pulled away. Minnie walked up to Philip and looked him over carefully. "I've missed you so much, Philip," Minnie said as she took Philip's face in her hands and kissed him on the cheek. "I'm so happy that you and Josie are here. I'm delighted to be a part of your special day."

Philip set down his packages, opened his arms, and gave his older sister a big hug. "I've missed you, too, Minnie. I'm so eager to catch up with you."

"Well, what are we doing standing in the yard! Let's go in the house. It's been a very long day for you. You must be tired. I'll let you get settled, and then we can sit down and catch up."

Philip took Josie's arm as they walked.

"Have you decided on a name for your new baby girl?" Minnie asked.

"We talked about it on the ride here. We decided to name her Mary, after our mother, Minnie. What do you think? Do you think that would have pleased Mother?"

Minnie stopped walking. She looked at Philip and smiled. She exchanged a quick look at Josie, who proudly held the pink bundle close to her body. "Yes, Mother would be very pleased."

"Is Arthur home?" Philip asked.

"No, but he'll be home from work soon. I started making dinner. You must be hungry. We'll eat as soon as Arthur gets home. I know he's looking forward to seeing you both and Mary, too." Minnie showed Philip and Josie to the guest bedroom. It was a large room with hardwood floors. The four-poster bed was covered with a bright red-and-white quilt. White open-lace curtains covered the windows that faced the large backyard. A small wooden cradle stood next to the bed. Philip immediately recognized the cradle as the one that his mother had used. He rubbed his hand on the curved railings of the cradle. Minnie had used it for her children.

"Do you recognize the cradle, Philip?" Minnie asked.

Philip glanced at Josie and pointed to the cradle. He nodded. "This is the cradle that Mother used. Seems hard to believe that I was small enough to fit in there, doesn't it?"

Josie walked over to the tiny cradle. "It's beautiful," she said as she touched the cradle with one hand. Carefully, she unwrapped Mary from the blanket and laid her in the cradle. She looked so peaceful. Josie gave the cradle a gentle push and watched it as it rocked slowly. "I can't seem to take my eyes off of her. We've wanted a baby for so long. Seems hard to believe that this day finally arrived."

Philip put his arm around Josie and gently pulled her close to his side. Tears came to Josie's eyes, and she made no effort to hold them back. Like the water in a flooding river, they welled and burst from their banks, trickling down her cheeks as she looked deeply into Philip's eyes. "I love you so much, Philip. I loved you from the moment I laid eyes on you the day that we met."

"Josie, you are the love and light of my life. I can't imagine my life without you." He held Josie's face in his hands, kissed her and then pulled her body close to his. "I'm the luckiest man in the world."

It had been a very long day. After dinner Philip and Josie retired to the parlor with Minnie and Arthur and talked until the sun went down. "I can't keep my eyes open one minute longer," Josie said. "I'm sorry, but I'm so tired. I think I'd like to give Mary another bottle before we go to bed." Minnie helped Josie warm some milk and prepare the bottle.

"Arthur will drive you to the depot in the morning. The train to Owatonna leaves at 9:00. He'll be sure to get you to the train in plenty of time. I'm sure that you're eager to get home."

"Thank you, Minnie, for letting us stay with you tonight. We appreciate your help. We miss you so; I wish that you didn't live so far away." They walked together to the guest bedroom with their arms around each other's waist.

After a hearty breakfast, Arthur took Philip, Josie, and Mary to the depot. They purchased tickets and made their way quickly to the train platform. They were very eager to return to Owatonna and get settled at home with their new baby. Philip took Josie's arm at her elbow and carefully helped her up the steps of the train car. The conductor peered inside the bundle Josie carried. "Oh, my, what a beautiful baby," the conductor said. "Is this her first train ride?"

"Yes, as a matter of fact it is!" Josie said emphatically with a big smile.

"Let's get on our way," the conductor remarked. "We don't want to keep the little lady waiting, now do we?" Within moments the whistle blew and the train pulled away from the station.

ഇ 5 ര

IT HAD BEEN EXCITING TO VISIT THE CITY, but Philip and Josie enjoyed life on their small farm in the quiet country much more. The city was too busy, too dirty, and too noisy. Philip and Josie gazed out the window as the train picked up speed. It wasn't long before the bright green countryside was whisking past them. Farm fields of corn and grain were lush with colors of green and gold. Leaves on the trees would be changing colors soon—a solid indication that it was time for the fall harvest.

The train arrived as scheduled at the depot in Owatonna. Philip and Josie were very glad to be home. They could see their buggy and horse waiting for them as they walked toward the livery. George, the livery owner, was at the front of the building. He was a thin, spry man, his skin weathered from working outdoors, his wiry gray hair stood out straight from the sides of his head. He was very personable and greeted everyone with the same wide grin. But this time his face was contorted, and he had a look of concern as he spoke.

"Philip, Josie, I'm glad you're back." George tipped his hat to Josie. "Looks like you got a new little bundle there." George cleared his throat. He looked down at the dusty street. "I'm sorry to have to tell you this, folks, but you need to go see the sheriff. Seems there's been a bit of trouble while you were gone. Willie's in jail."

Philip and Josie stopped short in their tracks. "What happened, George? What did Willie do?" Philip asked.

"Seems there was a fight at the saloon last night. Willie was there with the Nelson brothers. You know who the Nelson brothers are, don't you? I better not go on any more. Go see the sheriff and talk with him. He'll tell you what happened." The troubled look on George's face told Philip and Josie that something horrible had happened.

Philip and Josie were stunned. They hadn't expected this terrible greeting. They stood still and speechless. "We better go see the sheriff, Josie, and find out what kind of a fix Willie got himself into this time. George, we'll be back to pick up our things."

George hated to deliver such a terrible message. He could tell by the looks on their faces that he had ruined their special day. It was going to get worse for Philip and Josie, too, after they talked to the sheriff.

Philip and Josie made their way slowly towards the sheriff's office and the Owatonna jail. What trouble could Willie be in this time? He was a good young man, but he always seemed to find some sort of mischief or other, especially when he was in the company of the Nelson brothers. They had a bad reputation and had been in the Owatonna jail before.

The jail was a one-story, light-brown brick building on the same street as the saloon and other businesses on the main street of town. The sheriff's office was in the front of the building, and three small cells faced the alley at the rear. Anxiously Philip opened the door to the jail. He was afraid of what he might learn, and even more afraid to hear what the consequences might be. Willie must have committed some terrible offense or else George would have told him more about the incident. Josie walked quietly at Philip's side.

Sheriff Arnold sat behind a wooden table that served as his desk. A rack with several guns hung on the wall behind him. "Philip. Josie. Come in." Sheriff Arnold stood and extended his hand to Philip as they entered the room. He glanced at the bundle in Josie's arms. "I talked with George at the livery. He told me that you went to St. Paul to pick up your new baby. I'm afraid that I don't have very good news for you. Sorry, but I'm going to put a damper on your day." Sheriff Arnold was very solemn and spoke with a shaky voice. It was apparent from his demeanor that he had a very grave message to deliver. "Please come in and have a seat."

Philip and Josie sat on straight, wooden chairs across the table from the sheriff. The building was plain with no decoration. Bright sun beamed through the barred windows and cast unusual-looking shadows on the stone floor.

Sheriff Arnold, a good-natured man about forty-five years old, had been the sheriff in Owatonna as long as Philip could remember. He was well-liked and familiar with most of the town's residents. "Philip, Josie," Sheriff Arnold said nervously as he sat on the corner of the desktop. "Willie was with the Nelson brothers at the saloon last night. Seems they were drinking and playing cards quite a while. They left the saloon about dusk. They weren't gone too long when they returned to the saloon. They burst in the front door with guns drawn. Virgil Nelson and Willie kept their guns drawn and pointed at the patrons. LeRoy went behind the bar, stuck his gun in the ribs of Mr. Olson, the saloonkeeper. Mr. Olson gave him a sack of money. LeRoy grabbed it and struck Mr. Olson in the face with the butt of his pistol. He fell to the floor. LeRoy turned and shot him in the chest. He died immediately."

Philip and Josie couldn't believe what they heard. This had to be a nightmare that they'd wake up from. "I happened to be making my evening rounds in town and heard all the commotion at saloon. LeRoy, Virgil, and Willie came running out. I pulled my gun and shouted for them to raise their hands and stop. Willie and Virgil stopped. LeRoy ran with the bag of money in his hand. He didn't stop when I yelled to him, so I shot him." The sheriff lowered his head while he paused. "I'm sorry, but I shot him dead." Remorsefully, he continued. "I brought Virgil and Willie to the jail. They're in the cells in the back."

The story had gone from bad to worse. How could Willie be involved in such a horrendous crime? And Mr. Olson, the saloonkeeper, was a good man with a young family. His poor family. A million thoughts raced through Philip and Josie's heads.

"Sheriff Arnold," Philip said pensively. "Can I see Willie? Talk to him? I don't know what to say, but I would like to see him."

"This shooting is a much larger crime than the court in Owatonna can handle. I've contacted the State Prison in Stillwater. They'll be coming to take Willie and Virgil. They'll stand trial in Stillwater and probably be sent to the State Prison." Philip still couldn't believe his ears. Josie, too stunned to speak, squeezed Mary tightly against her body. "Philip, I'll take you to see Willie. Josie, do you want to come, too, or would you like to stay here in the office?" Josie didn't answer or even nod.

The sheriff led Philip to a hallway with a heavy wooden door. Several large keys hanging from a ring on his belt clanked and echoed in the narrow concrete hallway. The sheriff sorted through the keys and unlocked the cell door. Philip glanced back at Josie, who had begun to cry. She used the corner of Mary's blanket to wipe away her tears.

The jail cell was cold and damp. A small ray of light peaked through a narrow window at the top of one wall in the dark cell. Willie sat motionless on the edge of a thin, flat cot.

"Willie," Philip spoke through the narrow black steel bars of the jail cell. "Willie, look at me."

Dirty strands of long brown hair hung on Willie's face when he raised his head and looked at Philip. He shook his head perhaps at his own lack of bad judgment searching for the right words to tell Philip what he had done. "Looks like I'm in a real mess this time, huh?" Willie stared at the bare stone floor of the cell. "I'm in bad trouble."

"Yes, I'm afraid you are," Philip said. "Willie, how could you commit such a horrible crime? Mr. Olson was such a fine man. Now he's dead. How will his family survive without him? His poor wife. His poor children."

Quietly, Willie responded to Philip, "I never thought that LeRoy would shoot anyone. The plan was that we'd just take the money and leave town. Didn't think that anyone would get shot."

"Willie, I'm afraid that you're in the hands of the law now. I can't do anything to help you on this one. Sheriff Arnold said that someone from the State Prison is coming to get you and Virgil and take you to Stillwater. You'll stand trial there. I'll come to see you again before they take you away, but I have to leave now. Josie's waiting for me out front with our new baby. I have to take them home."

Philip turned and walked down the hallway with the sheriff back to the front. Willie's deep silence and lack of response made Philip think that it didn't matter to Willie if he came back to see him again or not.

ALL THE SPECIAL FEELINGS ABOUT BRINGING MARY home were diminished on their long, quiet ride to their small farm in the country. Their bright spirits were dampened by the sorry news of the crime that Willie had committed.

Josie fed Mary and placed her in a small cradle that Philip had made for her. Mary was a good baby who hardly ever cried unless she wanted to be fed or changed. She looked so peaceful in her cradle, so content and unaware of the trauma that Philip and Josie had faced with Willie. Philip came into the Mary's bedroom, which was flooded with brilliant sunshine. He gently placed his hands on Josie's shoulders. They both stared at Mary while she slept. "Josie we need to center our attention on our new lives with Mary. We've dreamed for years about having a baby. We've waited so long. She's finally here, and we can't let anything spoil this special time. We can't let Willie and his troubles take over our lives."

"I know, Philip, but I'm worried that the farm is too much work for you. You can't possibly do all the chores by yourself. Willie won't be here to help you with the crops. They're almost ready for harvest, and I won't be able to help you as much now that I have Mary to care for."

Philip put his finger under Josie's chin and lifted her head. "Maybe it's time we sell the farm. We've talked about selling before. I heard that they're looking for help at the Owatonna Foundry when I was in town last week. I could work at the foundry, and we could find a small house nearby if we sold the farm. I'll stop at the foundry and ask about a job the next time I go to town."

THE SMELL OF FALL WAS IN THE AIR. The colorful leaves on the trees glistened in the bright sunshine—shades of red, yellow, orange, and rust contrasted with the dark-green pine trees in the color-ful landscape. Crisp breezes whisked the leaves that had fallen. Unfortunately, it was just a precursor of the bitter-ly cold winter season just around the corner.

Josie worked dili-gently in the kitchen, pre-serving vegetables from her large garden. She gathered apples from the big tree that stood proudly in the backyard. Canned apple-sauce tasted so sweet in the dead of winter. Mary lay on

Marjorie at three months old.

a quilt on the kitchen floor while Josie worked around her. She was a good baby who easily entertained herself by grabbing at her stocking-covered toes or carefully examining her pudgy fingers. Mary rolled over

THEY NAMED ME MARJORIE

and got up on her knees. She rocked forward and back and then rested on her stomach again. She wanted to crawl, but hadn't quite figured out how. Josie hoped she'd wait just a little longer until she finished her fall canning and work in the kitchen. Preparing for winter involved substantial work, and she didn't want to have to chase a crawling baby, too.

Philip labored from before sunrise until after sunset. The days were getting shorter, which made it difficult for him to get all his work done before darkness arrived. The hay was cut but needed to be put up in the barn. Philip wished that Willie was there to help him, while he lugged heavy hay bales, one by one. An extra pair of hands would make the job much easier, much faster.

Philip worked until about noon. After lunch he went to town to pick up some supplies from the general store. Harry Brown, the owner of the store, greeted Philip at the front door. "Good afternoon, Philip. How are you? How are Josie and the new baby? I saw you at church on Sunday. That baby's growing like a weed." As usual, Harry wore a bright white apron and carried a pad of paper. A flat yellow pencil was wedged behind his right ear.

"Good afternoon, Harry. Josie and Mary are doing just fine. Mary's grown plenty in the past months. Now she's starting to crawl. Won't be long, I'm sure, and we'll be chasing after her." Philip paused briefly. "Harry, Josie and I want to sell the farm and move to town. The farm's too much work for me alone. Willie had his share of problems, but at least he usually helped me get the work done around the place. Without Willie, and Josie occupied with taking care of Mary, I can't get all the work done. I'm sure it'll be a hard winter for us. I heard there might be some job openings at the foundry. I'm going to stop there on my way home and see what work there might be."

"I'll keep you in mind Philip. Every now and then a new family comes to town and wants to settle here. Might have an interest in your farm. Yesterday, Harvey Stone, one of the foundry foremen, told me that they were looking to hire a few workers. You might get work if you stop over there. Good luck Philip. Say hello to Josie."

Philip paid Harry for the supplies that he purchased. "Give my best to Mrs. Stone."

BLACK SMOKE BILLOWED FREELY FROM TALL STACKS on the roof of the dirty-looking building that housed the Owatonna Foundry on the outskirts of town. Workers who pounded out parts for wagons from large pieces of metal also made repairs to wagons and large farm equipment. The foundry occupied the majority of the large building while a small office in the corner in the front faced the street. Large wagons and farm equipment were scattered around the perimeter of the building. Philip could hear the loud noise of pounding on metal when he parked the wagon in front of the building and approached the front door. He could see a weathered-looking, middle-aged man sitting behind a table littered with paperwork. *How did he ever find anything?* Philip wondered. The papers were soiled from the man's dirty, soot-colored hands. "Can I help you?" the man said as he shuffled papers and continued with his work.

"Yes, my name's Philip Sutton. My wife, Josie, and I live outside of town. We have a farm and fifty acres of land. We plan to sell the farm and move to town. Do you have any job openings?"

"Yep, we're looking for some workers. We seem to have more work than we can handle. What kind of experience do you have?"

Philip had learned to repair farm equipment while he worked side by side with his father on the family farm. "I've done plenty of farm equipment repair and welding. I'm willing to learn more, and I'm a hard worker."

Philip and the man talked in detail about the work at the foundry. The hourly wage was higher if Philip worked nights, which he didn't mind because it would allow him to spend more time with Josie and Mary during the day. Also, he could take odd jobs on farms in the area during the daytime if he needed more money. "How soon can you start?" the man asked.

"I'd like to get the crops up. Probably in about a month."

"Stop back the first of December, and we'll get you started. Here's some paperwork for you to complete. Drop it off next time you're in town."

Philip rushed home to tell Josie the exciting news of the job that he found. While he was in town he also located a small house to rent a short distance from the foundry and about a block from the Catholic Church, which had a school Mary could attend.

The following day, Philip talked to William and Emma Luke, who owned the farm to the north. The Lukes, who had four sons, were very interested in Philip and Josie's property, especially with the house, barn, and outbuildings. It would make a nice piece of property for their sons to own when they moved out. William told Philip how much he and Emma would miss him, Josie, and Mary. In their own way, the Lukes were good neighbors—the kind you could always count on when there was a need.

☙ 6 ❧

PHILIP AND JOSIE MOVED to the small, two-story sandstone brick house with brown shutters in mid-November. The house had three bedrooms—one on the main floor and two smaller bedrooms upstairs. The kitchen faced a large backyard with room for a vegetable garden and plenty of space for Mary to play. A small parlor at the front of the house and a porch looked toward the quiet street.

The work Philip performed at the foundry was dirty and strenuous. He usually arrived home tired and covered with soot from head to toe. The foundry was about a half-mile walk from their house, and because he worked the later shift, mid-afternoon to 11:30 p.m., he received more pay than the workers during the daytime.

Josie quickly became accustomed to life in town. She especially enjoyed seeing people during the day and getting to know the neighbors, some of whom had children about Mary's age. The children often played together in their backyard while Josie worked in the garden or hung the wash out to dry. Mary, almost five years old but small for her age, had curly yellow-blonde hair and bright blue eyes that twinkled when she smiled.

"Mary, come inside," Josie called to her. It's time to eat before your father goes to work." Mary grabbed her doll, Lizzie, and ran into the house. Mary never went anywhere without Lizzie, a doll that she received from Aunt Minnie and Uncle Arthur at Christmas. The doll had hair and closed her eyes when she was laid back. Mary held long conversations with Lizzie, her best friend. "Go wash up, Mary. Be sure to clean your hands with lots of soap."

"Lizzie and I were making mud pies in the yard. Maybe you and Papa would like one for dessert after dinner tonight," she said to Josie.

"Oh, I don't think so, Mary. Not tonight. I made your father's favorite, apple pie."

Philip came to the dinner table dressed for work. He would leave for work as soon as they finished eating. Mary and Josie were already seated.

"Let's bow our heads and say a prayer before we eat. Mary, will you start the prayer, please?" Mary bowed her head, her tiny hands in front of her like a church and prayed the prayer that they said together before every meal. Philip and Josie joined in. After the prayer, Josie filled Mary's plate and then passed the bowls of food to Philip who piled his plate high.

"I went to the post office today and collected our mail," Josie said. "We received a letter from Willie."

Philip looked up from his plate with a look of surprise. "We did?" he exclaimed.

"Who's Willie?" Mary said.

Josie and Philip looked at each other, wondering who was going to reply. They weren't expecting Mary's quick question. "Oh, Willie is a man who lived with us for a while when we lived on the farm in the country. You were only a baby at the time. You wouldn't remember him," Josie said.

Josie's response satisfied Mary's curiosity. She went back to her meal. Josie took the short letter from her apron pocket and handed it to Philip. Josie could tell by the expression on Philip's face that he had the same thought that she did after he read the letter. Willie sounded sad, said that he missed them, and invited them to visit him at Stillwater

State Prison. Prisoners were allowed visitors on Saturdays and Sundays. Philip folded the letter, put it back in the envelope and set it next to his plate. "Do you want to go visit Willie sometime, Josie?" Philip asked.

"I was waiting for your reaction to the letter, Philip, before I said anything."

"Are we going on a trip?" Mary asked. "Can I bring Lizzie with me?"

"We'll see," Josie said.

"Why don't you write a letter to Minnie in St. Paul? Let her know we're thinking about making a trip to Stillwater. Ask her if we could leave Mary with her for the day. We'll probably have to stay overnight and return the following day. I'd like to see Minnie and Arthur, too. It's been a long time." Philip thought about the day that he and Josie spent with Minnie and Arthur after they adopted Mary from the church home. It seemed hard to believe that five years could pass so quickly. "I wouldn't mind seeing Willie. After all, he was part of our family for a while." Philip paused. "Good boy. Just got mixed up with the wrong group of people. Sad thing."

MARY DIDN'T REMEMBER THAT SHE had been on a train before. Her mother told her that she had, but she had been far too young to remember. Josie thought back to their trip to St. Paul when she and Philip picked up Mary from the church home. She remembered how happy they had been when they brought their tiny baby home. It was a special day, one that she would never forget. Mary brought joy and new life to their house. Josie also remembered the bad news they had received about Willie just as they arrived home. It certainly dampened their spirits and put a dark cloud over their special day.

Philip and Josie wrote Minnie and received a letter back saying that she was excited that they were coming for a visit. Of course, she and Arthur would be happy to take care of Mary while they went to visit Willie at Stillwater. It would give them a good opportunity to spoil her, even if it was only a day.

Early on Saturday morning, Philip, Josie, and Mary walked to the train depot in Owatonna. The birds were just beginning to sing as the sun peeked through the trees and over the rooftops. "I don't think that I've ever been awake this early in the morning," Mary said. "It's so quiet. Where are all the people? Why do we have to leave this early?"

"The train ride from Owatonna to St. Paul will take a couple hours," Philip said. "Then your mother and I need to go on another train to visit an old friend of the family. You can stay with Aunt Minnie and Uncle Arthur. We'll be back about dinner time."

Mary had a look of concern on her face, and she clung tightly to Lizzie.

"Don't worry," Philip assured her. "Mary, you'll be fine. Aunt Minnie's my sister. You met her and Uncle Arthur when you were a baby, but you were too small to remember. Aunt Minnie will take very good care of you. I'm sure she'll do her best to spoil you rotten in a matter of a few hours."

Mary sat on her mother's lap when they boarded the train. She held Lizzie up to the window, so she could watch as the train pulled away from the station.

"All aboard!" the conductor yelled. "All aboard!"

The train moved forward with a jolt. Mary jumped and then rested again on her mother's lap. She watched the buildings in town as they whisked by. Within minutes the train was flying through the green countryside. A farmer was in the field cutting hay. Philip thought back to their life on the farm before they moved to town. Even though his job at the foundry was hard work, it was much better than life on the farm. When they lived on the farm, he never knew from one year to the next what the weather would bring and if he'd get a good crop or not.

Life on the farm had been difficult for Josie, too. She was slender and fragile. Although she tried, she wasn't able to do much work around the farm, especially after Mary arrived. Winters were particularly hard on her. She always got a chest cold or a cough that lasted most of the winter. Life in town seemed to be much easier on her.

The conductor asked to see the passengers' tickets as he walked down the aisle of the train car. He took Philip's tickets, punched them and handed them back to Philip. The conductor smiled and winked at Mary. She wasn't quite sure what to think about the man in the blue uniform with the funny looking hat.

"You're a cute little girl. How old are you?"

Mary looked quizzically at the conductor. She wasn't sure if she should reply.

"You can tell him, Mary," Josie said.

Mary held up five fingers and shyly replied, "I'm five years old."

"Is this your first train ride young lady?"

Mary nodded at the conductor.

"Have a good trip. I hope your friend has a pleasant ride, too," the conductor said as he pointed to Lizzie.

Mary squeezed Lizzie tight to her chest. She wasn't sure if she could trust the man in the blue uniform, and for certain she didn't want to lose her doll and best friend.

THE TRAIN PULLED INTO THE ST. PAUL DEPOT. Mary held her mother's hand tightly, as they stood up from their seats and walked down the aisle of the train car. Philip helped Josie and Mary down the steps and onto the sidewalk. "Well, Mary," Philip said, "what do you think about St. Paul?" Mary gazed at all the people moving quickly about. There were several trains chugging in and out of the depot, and people hurrying this way and that. Philip located a driver with a buggy and gave him the address of Minnie's house. They climbed aboard and the driver guided the horse out of the station.

Minnie greeted them at the front door of her red brick house when they arrived. "I'm so happy you're here," she said as she gave Philip a big hug. It's been so long since we've been together. I've missed you so. Josie, you look wonderful." Minnie glanced down. "Oh my, oh my, this must be Mary," Minnie exclaimed as she bent down to greet Mary.

Mary didn't remember meeting Minnie before. She pushed hard against her mother's leg while she grasped the end of her mother's long skirt in her hand.

"Mary, I'm your papa's sister Minnie. We met a long time ago, but I'm sure you don't remember me. You were just a tiny, tiny baby. My but you've grown. You are a beautiful little girl."

Mary wasn't sure if she should speak and just stared.

"I see that you brought a friend with you," Minnie said as she reached forward. Mary pulled Lizzie tight. "I'm not going to take your doll from you sweetheart. What's your doll's name?"

Mary looked up and shyly replied, "Lizzie."

"You and Lizzie look like one another. Has anyone told you that before? You have the same color hair and the same color eyes. Would you and Lizzie like to come to the kitchen for a cookie and a glass of milk? You must be hungry and thirsty. It's a long train ride from Owatonna to St. Paul."

They walked through the parlor and into the kitchen. The smell of fresh-baked bread permeated the house. Mary looked around as they passed through the rooms. She'd never been in a house this big. It was huge. They sat around the kitchen table while Minnie poured fresh-brewed coffee for Philip and Josie. She gave Mary a large glass of cold milk.

"Where's Arthur?" Philip asked.

"Oh," Minnie said, "he's working at the bank until noon. He'll be home for lunch."

"I'm afraid we won't be able to see him until we come back late today. I asked the buggy driver to come and get us in an hour to take us back to the depot. We'll catch a train to Stillwater and come back in time for dinner tonight," Philip said.

"Minnie, it's so nice of you to let us stay with you and Arthur. We appreciate your hospitality. We also appreciate that you offered to take care of Mary this afternoon while we go to visit Willie," Josie said.

"Oh, don't you worry. Mary and I will have fun while you're gone. I have some toys left from our children that she can play with. We can play out in the yard while you're gone. I think we may have a picnic," Minnie said. "What do you think of that, Mary? Do you think that you and Lizzie would like to have a picnic in the backyard?"

Mary was slowly warming up to Minnie. The cookie and glass of milk certainly helped, and the thought of a picnic appealed to her, too.

The buggy driver took Philip and Josie back to the train depot. They arrived just in time to catch a train to Stillwater. The thought of going to the State Prison made both of them very anxious. They had been to the Owatonna jail only once, when Willie was there with Virgil Nelson, after they robbed and murdered Mr. Olson, the saloonkeeper. The Stillwater prison, however, was a penitentiary for the entire state of Minnesota and had to be much larger. Philip and Josie weren't sure what to expect. When they arrived at the Stillwater depot, they went to the ticket window and asked for directions to the prison. The clerk pointed to the back of the building. "Go out the back door of the depot. You'll see the prison. It's the big, gray-stone building. You can't miss it. You can walk from here."

Philip and Josie immediately saw the huge gray-stone prison building surrounded by a tall black iron fence when they walked out the back door of the depot. The building overlooked the St. Croix River that separated Minnesota from the state of Wisconsin. A tall bridge, high enough to accommodate the frequent steamboat traffic, crossed the river.

Philip and Josie walked arm and arm up the street. "Philip, I'm scared," Josie said. "I'm looking forward to seeing Willie, but I'm afraid of the other men in the prison."

"Don't worry, Josie. I'm sure there are plenty of security officers. They're not going to let anything happen to us." Philip and Josie approached a small brick house at the edge of the prison grounds. An officer came forward. "May I help you? Who are you here to see?"

"I'm Philip Sutton. This is my wife, Josie. We'd like to see Willie Olmstead. We sent him a letter telling him that we planned to visit him today. We're from Owatonna."

"You had a long trip. Let me get a guard. He'll take you to a room where you can see the prisoner. First, though, I need you to sign your names. We keep a list of all the visitors to the prison and the dates and times of their visit. Security, you know." The guard stopped an officer of the prison when he walked by. "Would you please take Mr. and Mrs. Sutton to the meeting room? Then, bring Willie Olmstead to the room." Philip and Josie followed the guard through the black iron gates into the prison.

"I'll get Willie from his cell and bring him to you in a few minutes. Please be seated." A man in a gray uniform stood at the entrance of the room. He carried a large rifle in his hands. A prisoner, dressed in a striped uniform, sat with visitors at a table in another corner of the room.

It wasn't long before the door to the meeting room opened. Willie stood in the doorway with the guard behind him watching him intently. He wore a gray-striped prison uniform, and his hands and feet were bound with metal cuffs and chains. Willie was pale and very thin. His brown hair was cut short, and he was clean-shaven. Willie kept his head down and walked forward slowly. The guard pulled out a chair for him across the table from Philip and Josie. Willie seemed like an old man, although he was only twenty-five years old. The guard sat behind Willie, who coughed and wiped his nose on the sleeve of his thread-worn, soiled prison uniform.

"Philip, Josie, it's nice to see you again. Thank you for coming to visit me. I don't have any family or friends. I haven't had anyone come to see me since I was sent to prison. I'm glad you're here. It's nice to see you."

Philip and Josie were still stunned by Willie's appearance and found it hard to speak. Finally, Philip spoke. "Willie, it's been a long time. We should have come to visit you before, but we weren't sure if you wanted to see anyone. We also didn't know what restrictions the prison had regarding visitors for prisoners."

Josie couldn't take her eyes off of Willie. He looked so old. He wheezed and coughed when he breathed. "Willie, how have you been?" she said. "You look like you've lost some weight, and you sound like you have a cold." Willie coughed deeply and spit onto the floor.

"I haven't been well. I've had a cold for a long time, and it won't go away. I asked to see a doctor, but the doctor only comes to the prison every couple weeks and there are so many other prisoners who need to see him, too. Lots of us have this same cough. Seems that it just keeps spreading through the prisoners." Willie wiggled nervously in his chair and cleared his throat again.

"So, how ya been?" Willie said. "How's your little girl? I sure made a mess of the day you brought her home. That's one of the reasons that I wanted to see you. I want to apologize, tell you that I'm sorry for what I did. I knew that you were looking forward to going to St. Paul to pick her up. I was only thinking of myself. I should have stayed home that day like you asked and taken you to the train. Probably wouldn't be here today if I had done what you asked." Willie lowered his head and looked at his shoes. "I'm sorry, Philip and Josie. I'm sorry for what I did to you. You were good to me. I realize that now. I wish I would have realized it back then." He coughed and spit again. His face turned red, beads of sweat forming on his forehead.

"Willie, I think you have a fever. You're perspiring and you look chilled. I hope you get to see the doctor soon," Josie paused and thought about Mary. "We have a beautiful little girl. She's five years old. We named her Mary. She's a pretty little girl and very bright. She has yellow-blonde curly hair and shiny blue eyes that twinkle when she talks. We love her very much. We're lucky to have her as part of our family. We left her with Philip's sister, Minnie, in St. Paul while we came to visit you. It was her first train ride since the day we picked her up at the church home in St. Paul."

Mary Sutton at three years of age and standing in a chair.

Philip took a photograph of Mary from his pocket. He showed it to Willie. "It was taken when she was three years old."

"Oh, she's a cute little girl. I'm glad you got her," Willie said. "You deserve to have a child. I'm sure you're good parents to her. She's a lucky little girl."

The guard told Philip and Josie that their time was up and he had to take Willie back to his cell. The guard reached his big hand under Willie's arm and pulled him up to his feet. Willie's prison uniform was soaked with sweat from the fever.

"Thanks for coming to see me. It means a lot to me. You're the only family that I have. I'll never forget it."

Josie wanted to give him a hug. Instead, she put her hand on Willie's upper arm and rubbed it gently. As the guard moved forward, Josie quickly pulled her hand away.

"Take care, Willie. I hope you get better. I'm glad that we were able to see you." The guard escorted Willie from the room. When he reached the doorway, Willie turned and looked back at Philip and Josie. Tears filled his sad dark-brown eyes. Willie raised his cuffed hands to wave good-bye and then disappeared from view. Philip and Josie stood still, almost as stunned as they were when they arrived. Josie leaned her side up against Philip and rested her head on his shoulder. Philip squeezed her shoulder softly.

"Time for us to leave, Josie. We need to get back to the depot and catch the train to St. Paul." They walked out of the prison with without saying a word.

MARY RAN TO PHILIP AND JOSIE when they arrived at Minnie and Arthur's house. Lizzie dangled from Mary's hand by one arm. She was happy to see her mama and papa and tell them all about her day with her new friends, Aunt Minnie and Uncle Arthur. Mary was quick to show Philip and Josie the new black-and-yellow scarf that Minnie had knit for Lizzie.

"Look, Mama and Papa look," Mary cried. "See the scarf that Aunt Minnie made for Lizzie. Isn't it beautiful?" Mary wrapped the scarf around the doll's small body.

"Yes, it's beautiful, Mary. It was very nice of Aunt Minnie to make it for you. Let's go inside now. I think it's time for dinner." Philip, Josie, and Mary walked up the steps and into the house.

Minnie was making dinner in the kitchen. "Oh, Minnie, something smells wonderful. I hope that you didn't go to much trouble for dinner. Let me help you," Josie said grabbing an apron from a hook on the wall.

Minnie and Josie finished making dinner while Philip and Arthur talked in the parlor. Mary sat on the floor and played with Lizzie and her new scarf. After dinner they returned to the parlor and talked until well after dark. Mary fell asleep on the couch. Philip picked up her limp body in his arms and carried her upstairs, laying her on the bed that Minnie had prepared for her.

"It was so much fun to have Mary here today. She's a wonderful little girl. So full of life. Oh, and what a great imagination she has," Minnie said.

"We're very lucky to have her, Minnie. She's a blessing to us." Josie smiled softly.

Philip, Josie, Minnie, and Arthur sat at the table in the kitchen and played cards until it was time to go to bed. They had a good time reminiscing about the past. Josie tried to conceal a yawn with the back of her hand, but Minnie noticed.

"You've had a very long day today. I think it's time we all go to bed. We can visit a bit more at breakfast tomorrow before you need to catch the train back to Owatonna."

Philip, Josie, and Mary joined Minnie and Arthur for church services in the morning, and then went back to the house for a big breakfast. They took the afternoon train back to Owatonna. It was a wonderful visit to the city, but all the same it would be nice to be home again. Josie held Mary on her lap as the train departed the depot. Mary rocked Lizzie, wrapping the black-and-yellow scarf around the doll's neck and patting it in place. Josie stared blankly out the window. She couldn't stop thinking about Willie. His sad face and lonely expression was etched in her mind. The train whistle blew loudly and woke Josie from her daydream. They were in Owatonna. They were home.

ഌ 7 ൽ

I
T WAS A COOL, LATE SUMMER MORNING. Josie woke when Philip came home from work late at night. She tossed and turned the remainder of the night and finally slid out of bed early in the morning. Trying not to wake Philip, she put on a heavy wool sweater over her night dress and tip-toed quietly from the bedroom. This was Mary's first day of school. Mary had been so excited before she went to bed. Surely she would rise early.

Josie coughed several times. She had had a chest cold for a few weeks that she couldn't seem to shake. She lost her appetite and nothing tasted good. She lost some weight, which her slender frame couldn't afford and she couldn't keep her body warm, no matter how many layers of clothes she wore. Josie put the back of her hand to her forehead. It was warm, and she could tell that she had a slight fever. She planned to go see Doc Harms, if she didn't feel better in a couple of days.

"Mary, you look so pretty," Josie said as she tied a big blue bow in Mary's hair. "Be sure to listen to everything that your teacher says, all right?" Josie said. She spun Mary around and looked at her. Oh, she looked so grown up in her new dress and shoes. "Mary, why the long face? What's wrong?" Josie asked.

"I'm worried about Lizzie. Are you sure she can't go to school with me? She'll be real quiet. I can put her under my desk until it's time to come home," Mary said.

"Yes," Josie said. "I'm sure Lizzie can't go to school. You'll be so busy learning to read and making new friends at school that it'll be time to come home before you know it. I promise I'll take good care of her for you today. You'll have plenty to tell Lizzie when you come home this afternoon." Josie patted Mary on the top of the head. She started to say something, but started to cough instead. She took a drink of water. It helped for a moment, but then she started to cough again. Philip rose from bed in time to see Mary off to school. She looked so excited as she left the house. It was only a couple of blocks for her to walk to the Catholic Church that was a school, too.

"I heard you coughing this morning, Josie. You don't seem to be getting any better. I think you need to see Doc Harms."

"I know, Philip, I'll go tomorrow. I feel so weak and tired. I don't have any energy. I have a fever, too. I think I'll go back to bed for a bit. I didn't sleep very well last night. Maybe I'll get a bit of energy if I get a little more rest." Josie wrapped the wool sweater tightly about her thin body. She went to the bedroom, took a quilt from the rack, unfolded it, and laid in on the bed. She climbed under the covers and pulled them up securely around her neck.

Philip checked on Josie several times during the morning. She was sound asleep. He warmed some stew for lunch and took a bowl to Josie, but she never stirred. He decided to let her sleep a while longer. It wouldn't be too long before Mary would be home from school.

Philip was worried about his wife. She had lost so much weight and lacked energy. Her complexion was gray, and her eyes looked shallow and sunken into her face. Her lungs rattled when she coughed. He would be sure that she went to see the doctor tomorrow.

Josie got out of bed in the middle of the afternoon. She dressed and went out in the kitchen while Philip was making his lunch to take to work. "Oh, Philip, I can't believe that I slept all day. Why didn't you wake me? Here, let me get your lunch ready for you."

"I warmed some stew for you earlier. I took it in to you, but you were sound asleep. I'll get it for you." Josie stopped Philip when he went to get her the bowl of stew.

"Philip, I'm not hungry right now." Josie achieved a tiny smile, shaking her head. "I don't have much of an appetite. I'll wait until Mary comes home and have dinner with her. I wonder how her first day of school was. She was so excited when she left this morning."

Josie was seated at the kitchen table while Philip worked. She didn't have the energy to move. Moments later Mary burst in the front door, letting it slam behind her.

"Mama, Papa! I'm home." She ran into the kitchen and jumped onto Josie's lap. Philip walked over to the table and pulled out a chair.

"Come here, my big girl. Tell me all about your day at school."

Mary slid out of her mother's lap. She jumped onto her papa's lap. Josie felt awful. She wondered if she was going to have the energy to make dinner for Mary after Philip left for work.

When Philip came home from work that evening, Josie was sitting in the rocking chair in the dark bedroom. She wore a big wool sweater over her night dress and had a quilt wrapped around her. A half-empty glass of water sat on the floor next to the chair. Josie coughed loudly as Philip came in the room.

"Josie, what's wrong. Why aren't you in bed? You look awful." Philip touched Josie's forehead. "You're burning up. You're soaked with sweat. Here, let me help you back to bed."

"I can't lie down, Philip. I start to cough so badly as soon as I lie down. I feel better if I sit in the chair," she said.

"I better go get the doctor before you burn up," Philip said as he started to walk from the room.

"Philip, stop," Josie commanded. "It's only a few hours 'til daybreak. Let's not wake Doc Harms. You can get him when the sun comes up."

Shortly after daybreak Doc Harms walked into the bedroom. He was dressed in a dark suit and carried a small black bag. Josie was sitting in the rocking chair.

"Hello, Doc Harms," Josie said. Her voice was fatigued, grayish, like her appearance. The illness had drained her of color and energy, and it showed. "I'm sorry to make you come all this way. I should have come to see you earlier this week, but I thought I could get rid of this cold on my own. Guess I didn't do a very good job. Can you give me something to stop this terrible cough and get rid of the fever?" Doc Harms felt Josie's forehead. She was burning up.

"You need to get back into bed, Josie. Here, I'll help you." The doctor helped Josie stand and led her to the bed. He saw how thin she was when he unwrapped the quilt from her body. Josie crawled into bed. He fluffed the pillow and placed it under her head. Philip stood in the doorway while the doctor examined Josie. It wouldn't be long and Mary would need to get ready for school. It had been a long sleepless night. There was work that needed to be done—dirty dishes from Josie's and Mary's dinner the night before were in the dish pan on the counter, laundry hadn't been done for several days and was piled high. Philip could try to get a few things done before he went to work in the afternoon, but it would be a very long day at work if he didn't get at least a couple hours of sleep.

The doctor walked to the doorway where Philip stood. He shook is head. "Philip, I'm very concerned about Josie. She has a very high fever. We need to get her temperature down, or she'll burn up. I gave her some medicine that should help. I also gave her something to help with that cough. She's very sick. I think it's more than just a cold that'll run its course. Was she around someone else who was sick?"

Philip thought for a while. "Not that I remember," he said. "She always seems to get sick with a cold at this time of year. She's never had one this bad before."

"She needs rest. I took a sample of her blood. I'm going to take it to the hospital for tests. Perhaps that'll tell me something."

Philip gave a heavy sigh. The doctor patted his shoulder and walked toward the door. He glanced back at Philip. "I'll come back when I get the results of the tests from the hospital. In the meantime, be sure Josie gets rest. Try to keep her warm and comfortable. See if you can get her to eat something when she wakes up. We need to get her strength up."

The doctor let himself out of the house while Philip sat on the edge of the bed and watched Josie sleep. Her breathing was labored. Her chest made a rattling noise as she breathed in and out.

"Oh, Josie, please get better," Philip whispered as he stroked the top of her head. "I love you. Mary and I need you and want you to get well."

"Mary," Philip called. "Mary, where are you?" Mary came running from the backyard.

"What, Papa? I'm here."

"Mary, it's almost time for school. You need to eat breakfast. I'll help you. Then you need to get ready for school. You don't want to be late." Mary moved a small footstool over to the counter and stepped up on it. She washed her hands in a basin of water, splashed water on her face, and then wiped her face and hands with a towel. Philip put some mush in a bowl and poured Mary a glass of milk. He sat with her while she ate.

"Did the doctor make Mama better, Papa? How come she's still sleeping? Will she be better when I come home from school today?"

"Mary, Mama's very sick. I'm going to talk to Mrs. Olson today while you're at school. Maybe she can help me until your mama gets better. I need to go to work tonight, and you and Mama can't be alone."

"Me and Lizzie can take care of Mama while you're at work."

Philip sighed. Mary was growing up so quickly. Mrs. Olson lived just a short distance away. She and Josie had gotten to know each other while at church. Perhaps she could stay with Mary for a while and look after Josie while he went to work. Philip also wanted to stop in town and send a wire to his sister, Kate, who lived near Waseca. She might be able to come and stay for a while, at least until Josie got back on her feet. While at the post office, Philip checked to see if they had received any mail.

"Only one letter for you, Philip," Mr. Jones the postmaster said. He handed Philip an envelope. The return address was from the State Prison in Stillwater. Philip tore the envelope. The letter inside read: "With regret we inform you that Willie Olmstead died, August 18, 1903. Cause of death: Consumption. Burial at Stillwater, Minnesota. Philip held the letter in disbelief.

MRS. OLSON GREETED MARY WHEN SHE CAME home from school.

"Where's Mama? Is she better?" Mary said. She ran to the bedroom where her mother lay motionless in bed.

"Oh, Mary, your mama's very sick. She needs her rest. She needs to stay in bed. I'll get you supper and stay with you until your papa comes home from work."

A couple of days later, Philip received a wire from Kate. She would arrive the next day on the afternoon train. Doc Harms came to the house that day as well. He had a look of concern on his face when Philip met him at the door. Philip held the door to the house open as Doc Harms walked in. He carried a small black bag. "Doc, did you hear back from the hospital on Josie's tests. What did they say?"

"Can I see Josie?"

"Yes, come into the bedroom. She's still in bed. Can't seem to get the strength to get up."

Doc Harms sat at the side of Josie's bed. He touched her forehead. Josie stirred and opened her eyes.

"Doc Harms. How am I doing? What did the hospital say?"

"Josie, Philip. Yes, I heard from the hospital. I don't have good news. You have tuberculosis of the glands." Philip immediately thought about Willie. He hadn't told Josie about the letter yet. Josie may have contracted tuberculosis from Willie when they went to Stillwater to visit him.

"Josie, I can give you some more medicine. You need to get more rest. If you aren't doing any better in a couple days, we need to take you to the hospital if you think you're strong enough to make the trip. You need to keep Mary away. We don't want her to get sick, too."

Philip said, "My sister, Kate, will be here tomorrow. She'll help around the house and with Mary. It's been rough for me since Josie got sick. I've missed so much work, the foundry isn't very happy. They have more than enough work, and I don't want to lose my job."

The next day Philip and Mary met Aunt Kate at the train depot and took her to the house. She had a strong resemblance to Minnie. Philip welcomed her with open arms. He needed help with the housework and someone to look after Mary. Kate looked in on Josie but didn't want to wake her. "Philip, she looks so weak. She's lost so much weight. Can she even walk?"

"No, she hasn't gotten out of bed for several days. The doctor was here yesterday. Her tests came back from the hospital. She has tuberculosis. If she doesn't improve in the next couple of days, we'll have to take her to the hospital, if she can make the trip."

Kate looked at Josie. No way could a person this weak make it to the hospital. It was cold and snowy outside. The trip would only make Josie weaker.

Doc Harms continued to make daily visits to the house. Aunt Kate helped with the housework and looked after Mary. Josie's health continued to deteriorate. She was much too weak to go to the hospital. The doctor said the most that they could do was hope and pray that she would make a turn for the better.

Doc Harms left Josie's side and walked into the parlor. Philip and Kate followed him. "I'm very sorry. Josie's slipping away. There's nothing more that I can do to help her. It's just a matter of time."

Kate gently put her arm around Philip and pulled him close. He laid his head on her shoulder and started to cry. He loved Josie so much.

He couldn't imagine life without her. He wondered how he and Mary would survive without her.

Philip went to the bedroom and sat next to Josie on the bed. She didn't move. She was in a very deep sleep. He brushed the hair from her forehead and kissed her gently on the cheek.

Kate started with the housework as soon as she sent Mary off to school. She washed clothes, cleaned, and busied herself in the kitchen. The smell of fresh bread lofted through the house. *Poor Philip*, she thought as she worked. How difficult life would be for him without his Josie. How could he work at the foundry, take care of Mary, and the housework, too? It wasn't possible.

Later that day, while Philip was sitting at her side, Josie slipped away. She stopped breathing and quietly died. Kate went to get Doc Harms and brought him to the house. He said, "Philip, I'm sorry. She was too weak to recover. I did all that I could. I'm very sorry. You need to prepare for her funeral. I'll talk to Pastor Rogers on my way and let him know. He'll come to the house to talk with you."

Philip sat in disbelief. He put his face in his hands and sobbed a storm of tears. Kate stood in the doorway to the bedroom and wiped her own tears from her eyes with her apron. She hated to see her brother suffer such a terrible loss. And, how was he going to tell Mary that her mother died. She would be home from school soon. What was he going to say? Would she understand? Mary didn't know anyone who had died.

Philip met Mary at the front door of the house when she came home from school. He took her tiny hand in his, and they walked into the parlor. Philip sat on a chair and lifted Mary onto his lap. He held her close and started to cry. "Papa, what's wrong?" Mary asked. She had never seen her father cry before.

"Mary, Mary. Your mother was so sick. She just couldn't get better. While you were at school today, the angels came and took her to heaven. She's not coming back. She died." Mary looked quizzically at her father. Philip could tell that she didn't understand.

"Mary we need to get ready for her funeral. We need to figure out what we're going to do."

Pastor Rogers presided over the funeral at the church. Aunt Minnie and Uncle Arthur came from St. Paul. Aunt Kate's husband, Joe, came, too. The church was filled with people they had met since they moved to town.

It was a very cold and windy late fall day. Bare branches on the trees rattled in the wind. People huddled close to block the wind while dried leaves danced on the ground around the gravesite at the cemetery. After Pastor Rogers said the final prayer, they left the cemetery and went back to the house for a meal. Several people brought food to the house. Aunt Kate and Aunt Minnie worked in the kitchen. Mrs. Olson, who had cared for Mary during Josie's illness, held Mary on her lap. Mary clung tightly to Lizzie, her faithful companion who went everywhere with her. Mary was going to need that doll more now than ever.

Visitors offered their condolences to Philip. Late in the day, the house grew quiet as the last people left. Minnie and Arthur took the train back to St. Paul. Aunt Kate and Uncle Joe sat with Philip and Mary in the parlor. "Philip, it was a very nice funeral. The minister gave a wonderful sermon. I know it's not going to be easy on you; it'll take some time, but you'll adjust."

"Kate, I don't know what I'm going to do without her. I miss her already. How can I work and take care of Mary, too? How long can you stay?"

"I'll stay as long as I can. Maybe I can help you find someone to come to the house and help you and help care for Mary, too. Let's talk with Pastor Rogers after church services on Sunday. Maybe he'll know someone."

It was very difficult to go back to the church on Sunday where they had just been for Josie's funeral. Philip and Kate talked with Pastor Rogers after the service while Mary played with school friends outside under the big oak tree in the church yard.

"Philip, glad to see you at service today," Pastor Rogers said. "How are you? How's Mary getting along?"

"She seems to be adjusting better than I am. I miss Josie so much. I'm worried about how I'm going to make it without her. I can't care for Mary by myself, and Kate needs to go home to her family in Waseca. Do you know anyone who might be able to come to the house and help me?"

Pastor Rogers thought carefully and shook his head. "Maybe the Andersons. Perhaps Wilbur Anderson and his family could take Mary into their house for a while. They have a little boy about Mary's age. Also, there's the Clausen family that lives outside of town. It's a long way from here, probably ten miles or more. Mrs. Clausen's an invalid and uses a wheelchair to get around. Maybe they would be able to take Mary in. Mary's getting to the age where she might be able to help Mrs. Clausen, too."

Philip didn't like the thought of leaving his little girl with a family so far away. It would be difficult for him to visit her and she wouldn't be able to go to school, but it might be his only choice. Philip thanked Pastor Rogers and walked away.

During the following week Kate went to see Mrs. Anderson. The Andersons, who had five children, the youngest a small baby, lived at the far end of town. They wanted to take Mary into their home, but couldn't do it with the other children. It was difficult already with so many mouths to feed.

One day, Philip went to visit Ellen and Harvey Clausen, as Pastor Rogers suggested. They lived on a small farm about ten miles from town. Philip drove his horse and buggy into their yard near the front of the big house. Mr. Clausen, who was working in the barn, came into the yard when he heard the wagon pull in. "Can I help you," Harvey asked. "Are you lost? Looking for someone in these parts?"

Philip jumped from the wagon and tied the horse. He extended his cold hand. "Mr. Clausen, my name is Philip Sutton. I live in town, in Owatonna. Would you mind if I came in and talked to you and Mrs. Clausen. Pastor Rogers suggested that I come and see you."

"Sure, come up to the house. I'll get you something to drink. Sure is a cold day. Won't be long and winter will set in. I've been trying to get things ready before the first big snowstorm comes. By the looks of these gray clouds, probably won't be long."

They walked toward the big brick house. Philip looked at the lumber that covered the front stairs. Mr. Clausen noticed Philip's quizzical look. "My wife was in a horse-and-buggy accident a few years ago. She uses a wheelchair to get around. I need to get her in and out of the house, so I built the ramp over the stairs."

Mrs. Clausen came to the door to see who had come into the yard. She was a young lady about twenty-five years old. She used her hands to turn the big wheels of the chair which made creaking noises as it moved slowly. She pushed opened the big door and backed up as Philip and Mr. Clausen entered.

"Ellen," Harvey said, "this is Philip Sutton. He came from Owatonna. He knows Pastor Rogers." Harvey grabbed the handles of his wife's wheelchair and pushed her into the warm kitchen. "Mr. Sutton, this is my wife, Ellen." Ellen extended her hand to shake Philip's.

"Nice to meet you, Mr. Sutton. Would you like something to drink? I have some coffee. How about a piece of sweetbread that I made this morning. I used the last of the apples from our big tree in the yard."

"Thank you," Philip said. "A spot of coffee might be nice. It was a cold ride here. Looks like winter is just around the corner."

"Ellen, Mr. Sutton knows Pastor Rogers from the church in Owatonna. He sent Mr. Sutton to see us." Mr. Clausen poured steaming coffee from the pot into a cup and handed it to Philip. He grasped the warm cup and let the steam wash his face as he raised the cup to his lips.

"Mr. and Mrs. Clausen." Philip paused. He didn't know how to begin. He took another sip of coffee. In a tearful voice Philip started to speak again. "My wife, Josie, and I were married several years ago. When we learned that we couldn't have children of our own, we adopted a baby girl from a church home in St. Paul. Mary's six years old now. Josie died of consumption a few weeks ago." Philip lowered his head and paused again. He set his coffee cup on the table.

"I'm so sorry," Ellen said. "I'm so sorry. It must be very difficult for you. Poor Mary. I'm sorry for your loss."

"Yes, it must be terrible for you. Is there something that we can do for you? Is that why you came to see us?" Harvey asked.

Slowly, Philip pulled a tattered photo of Mary from his pocket and showed it to the Clausens. "This is a picture of my daughter Mary. She was three years old when it was taken. She's grown quite a bit since this picture was taken. She's a good little girl. She never causes a bit of trouble."

Ellen and Harvey stared at the picture of the little girl with the light-colored hair and bright eyes. "What a darling little girl. She's beautiful." Ellen smiled as she touched Mary's photo.

"It's been really hard for me since Josie died. I do repair work on wagons and farm equipment on the night shift at the foundry in Owatonna. My house is close to the foundry, but I can't leave Mary alone at night when I go to work. I'm looking for someone to take care of Mary until I can get back on my feet. Pastor Rogers suggested that I come to see you. He thought you might be able to take Mary in for a while. She's getting old enough now where she could help you around the house, Mrs. Clausen."

"Mr. Sutton, you have a beautiful little girl," Harvey said as he examined the photo. "She looks like she's full of life." He sighed softly and settled back in his chair. "I'm sorry I don't think that we can help you. My wife and I just found out that we're going to have our first baby in about seven months. With the new baby—well, I just don't think we can help you."

Ellen gave her husband a sympathetic smile. In a soft voice, she said, "Harvey, maybe we could let Mary stay here until the baby comes. It would give Mr. Sutton some time to get settled—perhaps he can find a permanent home for Mary in the next few months. She might be able to help me around the house. She can be my legs when I need help getting things. That would free you up some, too, because you wouldn't need to help me as much. Harvey, I think we should take Mary in for the coming months. Mr. Sutton, do you think you could find another home for Mary by next summer?"

"Congratulations, Mr. and Mrs. Clausen, you must be very happy about your first child. It would sure help me if you could take Mary, even if it's only until your baby arrives. It would give me some time to find a permanent home for her," Philip pleaded.

Ellen and Harvey exchanged thoughtful looks. Harvey poured Philip more coffee. Finally Harvey spoke. "All right, we'll take Mary in until the baby arrives."

Philip reached out and shook Mr. Clausen's hand. "Mr. Clausen, Mrs. Clausen." He nodded his head at each of them. "I'm very grateful. You're nice people. Pastor Rogers said that I would like you, and he was right. I appreciate your opening your home to my little girl. I'm sure you'll enjoy having her in your house. She'll be a big help to you, Mrs. Clausen. You'll see. When would you like me to bring her to you?"

"As soon as you like, I guess," Mr. Clausen said. "Looks like we're starting our family a bit sooner than we expected," he exclaimed.

Ellen smiled sweetly. "I can't wait to meet her. I'm sure she'll like living on the farm. There's plenty of room to run and play outside. Some difference from living in town, I would imagine."

"Yes, I do believe you're right. I better get going—want to make it home before it gets dark. I'll gather Mary's things up and bring her to you after church on Sunday. Is that all right with you?"

"Yes, that would be fine. It will give us a few days to get a room ready for her. She can use one of the bedrooms upstairs," Ellen said. Harvey and Ellen's bedroom was on the main floor of the house and their baby would stay in their room in a cradle, at least at the beginning. Ellen wasn't able to go up the stairs, but Harvey could help Mary if she needed anything in her room.

Philip walked to the door. "Mr. Clausen. Ma'am. I can't thank you enough. I'll come back on Sunday with Mary. God bless you." He made his way down the ramp and boarded his wagon. He waved at Mr. and Mrs. Clausen as he drove out of the yard.

Even though Philip liked Mr. and Mrs. Clausen, he felt that he had no choice, and it was going to be very difficult to leave Mary with them. He asked himself what he could have done differently and he thought hard about how he was going to tell Mary about her new home and wondered how he would adjust to living without her, too. She had become the light of his life since Josie died. He hoped she would understand that it was only temporary, that he planned to bring her back home with him just as quickly as he could.

๑ 8 ๙

SATURDAY AFTERNOON WAS COLD. Flakes of snow whisked though the chilly air. They melted, however, as soon as they hit the ground. That night after dinner Philip sat in his chair in the parlor while Mary played on the floor with Lizzie in front of the fireplace. The room contained a couch and a couple arm chairs with a small table between them that held a colorful glass lamp that Philip surprised Josie with the year before at Christmas. Curtains were tied back from the large window that faced the street at the front of the house. "Mary, bring Lizzie and come sit on my lap, would you please?" Philip asked.

Mary grabbed her doll with the black-and-yellow scarf wrapped securely around its body. She crawled onto her papa's lap. She laid Lizzie on her lap and watched the doll's eyes close while she stroked the doll's ragged hair. "Mary, I know you miss your mother very much and I miss her a lot, too. It's been very hard for both of us since she died. I'm sure the angels in heaven are taking very good care of her. She's not sick anymore, and she isn't suffering either." He choked back the tears as he talked. This talk with Mary was much more difficult than he thought. He had practiced what he planned to say many times but the words didn't come as easily as he thought they would. He held Mary tight.

"I miss Mama, too, Papa. So does Lizzie. Mama used to read to me. I liked it when she would put me to bed at night. She would sit on my bed and sing to me until I went to sleep." Mary started to hum one of the songs that her mother taught her. "How come you never sing to me, Papa?"

"I guess that's one of those things that mamas are good at, not papas." He gently put his finger under Mary's chin. He lifted her head and looked into her bright blue eyes. They twinkled like shining stars. "Mary, I met some very nice people the other day. Their names are Mr. and Mrs. Clausen. They live in the country on a farm not too far from here." He couldn't believe what he was about to say. "I went to their house in the country. They have cows and chickens on their farm. Oh, and they have a dog with white and black spots. He has one big spot over his right eye. His name's Dakota."

"That's a funny name. I've never heard of a dog named Dakota."

"He seemed like a real nice dog. He licked my hand when I reached out to pet him. He wagged his tail so fast that I thought it might fall off."

"Do you think that could happen, Papa?"

"No, I don't think so." Philip smiled. "Mr. and Mrs. Clausen said that I could take you to their house to stay for a while. Mrs. Clausen wants to help me take care of you. I showed Mr. and Mrs. Clausen your picture. They're looking forward to meeting you."

"Are they coming to visit us, Papa? They could come for dinner tomorrow after church."

"No, Mary. They aren't coming here. We're going to their house tomorrow after church services. They said that you can live with them at their house on the farm for a while, at least until I find someone to help me with the housework and cooking. I need someone to care for you because I can't leave you alone at night when I go to work."

"But Papa, I don't want to leave my house. I don't want to leave you. I'll get lonesome for you." Mary started to cry and tried to wiggle her way out of Philip's arms. He held her tight.

76

"Mary, I'll miss you, too. It's just for a short while. You'll like Mr. and Mrs. Clausen. They're very nice people. You can bring Lizzie and your other toys with you."

Mary started to cry. "I don't want to leave you, Papa. Don't take me away from you, please." She rested her head against his shoulder.

"Tomorrow after church I'll get the wagon ready. I'll pack a bag for you with your clothes and your toys, and, of course, Lizzie will come, too. We'll have to bundle up warm. It'll be a cold ride."

Mary snuggled on her papa's lap and cried softly. She fell asleep in his arms. Philip carried her up the stairs. He laid her on the bed while he untied the blue ribbon from her hair and placed it on the bureau. He took the tiny shoes from her feet and set them at the foot of the bed. Gently, he removed her dress and pulled her nightgown over her head. She woke, then fell back to sleep immediately. Philip laid her under the covers and tucked them tightly about her. He rested Lizzie at her side, then he sat on the side of the bed and quietly hummed a song—nothing like Josie used to sing, he was sure.

On Sunday, after church services and dinner at home, Philip loaded the wagon. He went inside to get Mary, but she was nowhere to be found. The floor squeaked as Philip walked to Mary's room on the second floor of the house. "Mary, where are you?" he called. "It's time to leave." He slowly pushed open the door to her room. Mary was dressed in her best Sunday dress. Her coat, hood, and mittens waited at the end of the bed. Lizzie lay on her lap.

"Papa, my room's so empty. All of my clothes are gone. All of my things, my toys. Do I have to leave you? I don't want to go."

"Mary, we don't have a choice. It's time to go." He held out his hand. Mary ignored his offer to help as she climbed off the bed. She laid Lizzie on the bed while she put on her coat. She picked up her doll, hood, and mittens and walked slowly past Philip and into the hallway. She didn't look back.

The crisp wind bit at their skin on the very long cold ride into the country. Mary, covered by a warm quilt, sat close to her papa and felt the warmth from his body. Black leafless tree branches swayed in the wind and big snowflakes floated through the frosty air. An occasional flake came to rest on Mary's mitten. She examined each flake carefully because she had learned in school that no two snowflakes were alike. The snowflakes blew off her mittens before she had time to decide.

"Mary, look. That's your new home." Philip pointed ahead of them as a farm and red-brick house came into sight on the horizon. "See it? The red-brick house up there a ways. Do you see it?"

Mary looked down at the floor of the wagon; she didn't want to look. Maybe if she didn't see the house it wouldn't happen. Her papa wouldn't leave her.

"Look, Mary, I see Dakota. Look, can you see the dog playing in the yard?"

Mary pushed the hood from her forehead as she lifted her head very slowly. She caught a glance of the black and white dog that was barking and jumping playfully with a man who was walking to the barn. They were getting very close to the house.

"Mary that man is Mr. Clausen. He's a very nice man. I met Mrs. Clausen, too. You'll like her, you just wait and see. You'll be very happy here. They'll take care of you, just like . . ." Philip paused and didn't finish the sentence. Memories of Josie flashed through his mind. Why did she have to die? Why couldn't their lives be the way that they used to be?

Mr. Clausen came out of the barn as Philip drove the wagon into the yard. He helped Philip tie the horse's reins to a wooden post at the edge of the rail fence. Mr. Clausen looked at Mary on the seat of the wagon and smiled.

"This must be Mary. Hello Mary," he said as he reached out his hand toward her. "It's very nice to meet you. Let me help you down from the wagon."

Mary fixed herself hard on the wagon seat while fear rang in her heart. Philip noticed her apprehensive look. "Mary, I'll help you down. Hold tight to Lizzie."

Mary held Lizzie in her right hand and raised her arms into the air. Philip lowered her to the ground. Mary stood tightly against her papa's leg. "Mary, this is Mr. Clausen." Just then the black and white dog with its long ears flopping came running up to Mary. He wagged his tail so hard that he could hardly walk. He paused to lick Mary's mitten.

"Oh, I can see that you're going to be good friends. Dakota likes you already. Look at his tail wag. That's how he says that he likes you."

Mary smiled weakly.

"Let's go into the house and get out of the cold. I think Mrs. Clausen will have something for you to drink that'll warm you up. Come inside."

Philip grasped Mary's hand as Mr. Clausen led them up the ramp and into the house. Mary looked at the wood that covered the steps; she had never seen funny-looking stairs like these. Steam rose from the pot that Mrs. Clausen stirred on the wood burning kitchen stove while she sat in her wheelchair.

"Thought you might like some warm soup after your long ride." Mrs. Clausen turned from her work at the stove as they came through the door. "Please take off your coats and have a seat at the table. The soup is nearly done."

Mary stood frozen like a statue with her mouth wide open. She had never seen anything like the chair that Mrs. Clausen used. It had wheels! It moved! Mary was astonished when Mrs. Clausen rolled across the kitchen floor and close to Mary, who was still clinging to Philip.

"You must be Mary. I'm very happy to meet you. May I help you take off your coat?"

Mary handed Lizzie to Philip and took off her mittens, hood, and coat. She handed them to Philip and took Lizzie back while glaring the entire time at the woman in the funny-looking chair.

"What's your doll's name, Mary? She has beautiful hair. Oh, and I see her eyes close, too, when you lay her back."

Mary spoke firmly in a solid voice. "This is Lizzie. She's my doll. I've had her since I was a baby. We go everywhere together."

"I see that. She has a beautiful scarf too."

"Aunt Minnie knit the scarf for me when we went to visit her and Uncle Arthur in St. Paul. We took the train to their house." Mary still couldn't manage to take her eyes off the unique chair that Mrs. Clausen used to maneuver about in the kitchen. Mary's curiosity finally peaked, and suddenly she blurted, "Mrs. Clausen, why do you sit in that chair? It has wheels."

"Shhh, Mary," Philip said as he patted Mary on the top of her head. "That's not a nice question to ask."

Mary didn't understand what was wrong with what she said. Mrs. Clausen turned and smiled kindly at Mary and Philip.

"Oh, it's all right. I get asked that question all the time. Many people haven't seen a wheelchair before." She rolled closer to Mary so she could get a better look at the chair. "I was in an accident with a horse and buggy a couple years ago. I was hurt really bad, and I can't use my legs anymore. I can't walk. The doctor gave me this chair so I can get around better."

The answer satisfied Mary, but she still couldn't take her eyes off the chair. *What an ingenious way to move about*, she thought.

Steam billowed from bowls of hot soup that Mrs. Clausen placed on the dining table. The Clausens and Philip talked while Mary gazed at the big backyard she could see through the kitchen window on the other side of the room. Dakota was chasing a yellow cat that passed through the yard on its way to the barn. *It might be fun to have a dog to play with*, Mary thought, *especially one as playful as Dakota.*

"Mr. and Mrs. Clausen, I can't thank you enough for taking care of Mary for me. I'm sure she'll be very happy with you, and I know that you'll take good care of her. Mary's a very good girl and will be able to help you, too. Won't you, Mary."

"Yes, I will. I used to help Mama with the housework when she was sick until she died." Suddenly there was a haunting silence in the room. No one knew what they could possibly say to help heal Mary's pain of losing her mother.

"Mr. and Mrs. Clausen, I brought some of Mary's things; they're in the wagon. I'll get them and bring them in, if that's all right," Philip said.

Mr. Clausen pushed his chair away from the table. "I'll help you get Mary's things, and then we can show Mary where her new room is." Mr. Clausen and Philip went to the wagon and came back with a couple bags. "Mary, would you like to see your room? It's upstairs. Come follow me." Mary wasn't too sure that she wanted to follow Mr. Clausen. "I'm sure you'll like your new room, Mary. It has a big window that looks over the side yard, which has a big oak tree that I plan to put a swing in just as soon as the weather warms up. We put new lace curtains on the window and a new feather tick on the bed, too."

Mary hopped down from the chair at the dining table, grabbed Lizzie by the arm and followed the men up the stairs to the second floor of the house. Mr. Clausen pushed open the door to her room at the end of a short hall. Mary peeked inside. There was a bed with a big feather tick on it, a bureau, and a closet. Bright sunshine streamed through the window that faced the yard. The room seemed to be about the same as any other room. She went over to the window and looked outside. Dakota was snooping near the barn, probably looking for that cat that had hidden safely inside. Mary stood silently and wondered what it was going to be like living on a farm. She knew that she lived on a farm with her mama and papa when she was a baby, but she couldn't remember what it was like. She couldn't see another house or farm as far as she could see in the distance. All she could see was flat bare farmland.

Mr. Clausen and Philip set Mary's bags on the bed. "I'll help you get settled later Mary," Mr. Clausen said as Mary continued to look out the window. "What do you think of your new room?" Mary turned away from the window and very politely replied, "I like it fine, thank you."

Philip bent down and rested his knees on the hardwood floor. He put his strong hands on Mary's tiny shoulders and looked in her sad eyes. "Mary, you'll be very happy here with the Clausens. They'll take good care of you until I can come get you and bring you home and we can be together again." Mary hugged Philip tightly around the neck.

"Papa, I'll miss you so much. Please hurry back and get me, so I can live at home."

Philip rose from his knees.

"It's time for me to leave, Mary." Hesitantly, he walked from the bedroom. He paused in the doorway. The image of Mary's sad face was etched in his mind. Next to burying Josie, this was the most difficult thing he ever had to do. He was sure this was best for Mary, though. He knew he couldn't care for her on his own. He would keep his promise to her and come get her and bring her home again. He went down the stairs to the kitchen where Mrs. Clausen cleared the lunch dishes from the table and moved them to the counter near the basin.

"Did you find everything all right?"

"Yes, it's a fine room. It's time for me to leave. Thank you again for taking care of Mary for me. I'll be back to get her in the spring of the year." He put on his coat and picked up his hat. "Mrs. Clausen, thank you," he said as he tipped his hat. He put his left hand firmly on Mr. Clausen's shoulder and shook his other hand. "Thank you for helping me out, Mr. Clausen." Philip walked out of the house and down the ramp to his wagon. He boarded the wagon and never looked back. Lizzie dangled by one arm from Mary's hand as she stood on the ramp at the front of the house and waved to her papa, who continued to look straight ahead as he drove down the road.

"Mary, come into the house. It's cold outside, and you don't have a coat on. You'll catch your death of cold." Mary watched her father's wagon until it was out of sight.

Mr. and Mrs. Clausen welcomed Mary into their home. She was a big help to Mrs. Clausen and served as Ellen's legs, often doing things for her as she sat in her wheelchair.

Mary liked living on the farm but missed the company of other children and people. Everything was very far away. It was a long ride in the wagon to town. They went to church on Sundays when the winter weather allowed. Before long, the snow started to melt. Winter's end was in sight as the days grew longer. Spring was on its way. It wouldn't be long and the weather would be much more suitable to enjoying the out of doors.

Mary missed her papa. She hadn't seen him since that sad November day when he left her at the Clausens'. She wondered if he would ever come back and take her home. Had he forgotten her? Sometimes she wondered if she was going to stay with the Clausen's forever. At times she would close her eyes hard and try to see her papa's face. She could see the shape of his face and his mustache, but the rest of his image was faint. Oh, how she longed to see him again.

One day, while eating dinner, Mrs. Clausen announced that she and Mr. Clausen were going to have a baby. The baby would probably arrive in May or early June. Mary was excited by the big news. It would be fun to have a baby in the house, more company for her and Lizzie.

"Will it be a girl baby or a boy baby?" Mary asked.

Mrs. Clausen smiled and said, "It'll be a surprise. We'll just have to wait and see. The baby should be here shortly after your birthday in May." Mary silently hoped it would be a baby girl.

Mary, almost seven years old, hadn't even thought about her birthday that was soon to arrive. She remembered how special her mama had made her birthday one time. They had eaten a delicious cake while her mama and papa sang a happy birthday song to her. It was a very memorable day. She wondered if she would ever be part of a family again with a mama and a papa. Sometimes, in the night, she even dreamed of it.

"OH, HARVEY. LOOK AT HER LITTLE FINGERS. Oh, and her toes are so tiny. She's so perfect." Ellen examined the tiny baby in her arms while Harvey sat on the edge of the bed. It was early-June, and the baby had arrived right on schedule.

"I'd like to name her Helen, after my grandmother. What middle name should we give her?" Ellen asked.

"How 'bout Lucille? She can have my grandmother's name for her middle name."

"Helen Lucille Clausen. I like it. It's a perfect name for a perfect baby."

Mary played with Dakota in the yard until the doctor left before she went into the house. The doctor told her that a baby girl had arrived. So, she got her wish—a baby girl. Not really a sister, but at least a baby girl.

Mary walked up the wooden ramp and into the house. Mr. and Mrs. Clausen's bedroom door was cracked open. She saw Mrs. Clausen lying on the bed. Mr. Clausen was looking at the baby wrapped in Mrs. Clausen's arms. Mr. Clausen saw Mary peeking into the room. "Would you like to take a look at the baby? It's a girl. Would you like to see her?"

Carefully, Mary walked into the bedroom. Mrs. Clausen smiled at her. "Look, Mary. Come see our baby daughter."

Mary leaned over the bed and looked at the baby's red face and dark hair. "She's so little," Mary whispered. "She's hardly any bigger than Lizzie!"

Mr. and Mrs. Clausen smiled. "You're absolutely right, Mary! We named her Helen Lucille."

"Mary, we need to let Mrs. Clausen rest for a while. The baby—I mean Helen—is sleeping, so it's a good time for her to rest. Won't be long and I'm sure that Helen will want to eat." Mr. Clausen slid the baby's cradle next to Mrs. Clausen at the side of her bed. He took Helen from her arms, laid the baby gently in the cradle and covered the baby with a small patchwork quilt. The cradle rocked back and forth slowly when he gave it a gentle touch. Mrs. Clausen rested her head on the pillow and looked over at the baby.

"Shhh, Mary. Let's let them sleep. We'll come and look in on them again in a little while."

IT WAS A BEAUTIFUL JULY SUMMER DAY. The sun was bright with not a cloud in the sky. Why couldn't every day be like this? It was absolutely perfect.

Helen rested on Mrs. Clausen's lap while she sat in the yard in her wheelchair. Mrs. Clausen took a diaper from the laundry basket, shook it and handed it to Mary. Mary hung it on the line with wooden clothespins that she took from the bag on the side of Mrs. Clausen's chair. They continued to hang laundry on the line until the basket was empty.

"I think it's time for lunch, Mary. Would you get Mr. Clausen? He just came from the field and went into the barn. Ask him to come inside, and we'll have something to eat. Helen's getting hungry, too."

Mr. Clausen put the horse in its stable and shut the door as Mary walked into the barn. "Mrs. Clausen said it's time to come into the house for lunch."

"Good, I'm hungry. How about you?"

Mary agreed, and they walked out of the barn together. They paused when they heard the noise of a horse on the road at the edge of field. Mr. Clausen and Mary turned to look at exactly the same time. Clouds of dust lifted from the horse's feet as the man rode it up the dirt road leading to the house. All of a sudden, Mary realized that the man riding the horse was her papa. She couldn't believe her eyes—was it real or was she having a dream? Mary stood motionless while she confirmed what her eyes saw. It was Papa.

"Papa!" Mary screamed. "Papa! Papa!" Mary ran as fast as her tiny feet would carry her small body. Her heels kicked at her backside and her arms spread wide open. "Papa, you're back! You came back! I thought I'd never see you again." Her heart swelled, and tears of joy ran down from her bright blue eyes.

Philip dismounted the horse. Mary flew into his wide open arms. He hugged her tightly, pushed her head against his chest and rubbed his cheek against the soft curls on the top of Mary's head. Tears flowed freely down his dusty face.

"I thought I'd never see you again, Papa. I thought you forgot about me," Mary cried.

"Mary, I'd never forget you. I told you that I would come back for you." Philip pushed Mary out at arm's length and looked at her. "You're my little girl. Just as I remember, only so much bigger. My how you've grown." He pulled her to his chest and gave Mary another hug. He lifted her chin with his big finger, looked at her teary eyes and asked, "Would you like to come back home to live again?"

"Oh, Papa!" Mary exclaimed. I'll go get Lizzie right now." She tried to get out of her father's embrace, but he held her tight.

"Wait, wait, wait. Not so fast little lady. I didn't mean this second. I need to talk with Mr. and Mrs. Clausen. I thought that I should let them know about my intentions today. If it's all right with them, I'll come back and get you on Sunday after church. Let's go talk to them now."

Philip took the reins of the horse in one hand and Mary's hand in the other. They walked slowly up the road to the house. Mrs. Clausen sat in her wheelchair on the ramp at Mr. Clausen's side. She held Helen in her arms.

"Mr. Clausen." Philip extended his hand and shook Mr. Clausen's. "Mrs. Clausen," he said as he took off his hat. "I see you have a new little baby." He bent over and looked a little closer.

"Yes, she was born on June 2. We named her Helen Lucille. She's been a very good baby. Mary's been helping me care for her. She's been a big help to me."

"I bet she has been," he said as he smiled down at Mary. "You have a beautiful baby girl." He thought for a moment. "Mary, I remember when you were that small. It was a long time ago."

"What a nice surprise to see you Mr. Sutton. Please, come in the house. We're about to have lunch. Please join us."

Mr. Clausen opened the door and pushed Mrs. Clausen inside. Mary and Philip followed them into the kitchen. Mary put the dishes on the table and then brought a plate of bread and sliced meat to the table. Mrs. Clausen pulled her wheelchair up to the table. Helen rested quietly on her lap.

Mary listened quietly as Mr. and Mrs. Clausen talked about the long cold winter. They talked about the crops Mr. Clausen had planted. It was a dry summer so far. A bit of rain would be most welcome and would help the crops.

Mary couldn't stand being quiet any longer. She sat straight in her chair and blurted, "Papa came here to take me home. I'm going home with him on Sunday after church." Mr. and Mrs. Clausen sat quietly. Helen stirred on Mrs. Clausen's lap and sounded a little whimper. It was getting close to her lunch time, too.

"Mary, shhh! Quiet, please! I need to ask Mr. and Mrs. Clausen if it's all right with them first."

Mary sank in her chair. What if they said no? Do you suppose they wouldn't let her go home with her papa?

"Mr. and Mrs. Clausen," Philip started slowly. "I came here today to talk to you about taking Mary home to live with me again. Several months ago I told you that I needed to get my life straightened around after Josie died. I think I've done that now. I married a couple of weeks ago. My new wife is Sarah—Sarah Doolittle." Mary's eyes opened wide. She stared at Philip. She wasn't exactly sure what to think or say.

"Sarah's new in town. I met her while I was at the general store one day. Her son, Henry, is eighteen years old. When Sarah's mother was widowed last year, she moved in with Sarah and Henry. Sarah and Henry moved in with me into our house, and we found a room for Sarah's mother to stay in at the house across the street from us. Sarah likes having her mother nearby."

Mary continued to listen to her papa talk about his new wife and her family. Not only did she have a new mother but a brother and a grandma across the street. She never had a grandma before, only aunts and uncles.

"If it's all right with you, Mr. and Mrs. Clausen, I'd like to come back on Sunday to get Mary and take her home. That'll give her a couple days to get her things packed. Time for you to say good-bye, too."

Mr. and Mrs. Clausen looked at each other and nodded in agreement. Mr. Clausen said, "Sounds all right to us. We'll have her ready for you on Sunday."

"Oh, Papa. I'm going home. I can't wait to be with you again." Mary hopped down from her chair. She stood next to Philip. He pushed his chair away from the table and pulled her up on his lap. He squeezed her around the middle.

"Yes, it'll be nice to have you at home again, too, Mary. I've missed you."

It seemed like an eternity until Sunday finally came. Philip returned with the horse and buggy to pick up Mary early in the day, just as he had said. Mary had all her things on the bed ready to go. Philip helped her pack them in the travel bags he had brought. Mr. Clausen helped Philip load Mary's bags into the wagon. Then Mary carried Lizzie and her black-and-yellow knitted scarf.

"Good-bye, Mrs. Clausen," Mary said as she gave her a big hug. "I hope I can come back and visit you. I said good-bye to Helen already. I'd like to see her when she gets bigger. Maybe we could play together sometime."

"Good-bye, Mary. Hurry on, now. Your papa's waiting at the wagon to take you home."

Mary ran down the wooden ramp. She hadn't stopped running when Philip grabbed her at the waist and lifted her onto the wagon seat. Mary rested Lizzie on her lap. Philip shook Mr. Clausen's hand and then boarded the wagon. With one snap of the reins the horse pulled the buggy down the road and to their home in Owatonna.

✼ 9 ✼

EVERYTHING IN THE TOWN WAS JUST as she had remembered. Not much had changed. Mary recognized the church and school that she attended. In the distance, at the end of the street, she caught a glimpse of their house. It looked exactly the same. Home at last. Shivers filled her body, even though it was a very warm summer day.

Philip pulled the wagon up to the house and stopped.

"Are you ready to meet your new mama?"

Mary didn't exactly know what to say. No one would ever be able to be her mama. Her mama died. "Yes, Papa. I'm so happy to be home."

Philip helped Mary from the wagon. He grabbed a couple of her bags while Mary examined the backyard. Apples were growing on the tree, just as she had remembered. Philip followed Mary into the house. A large woman stood near the counter on the other side of the room.

"Mary, this is my new wife." The woman walked toward Mary and Philip. "Sarah, this is Mary."

"Hello." Sarah looked at Mary, up and down. She examined Mary closely from all sides. It made Mary uncomfortable to have this strange woman looking at her so carefully. "Your papa's right. You sure are a little one. How old are you?"

Mary glared back at the curious woman. Confidently she answered. "My name is Mary Sutton. I turned seven years old on the seventeenth of May."

"Oh, you really are a little bit of a thing, aren't you?" Sarah continued looking down at Mary. The woman was very tall, almost as tall as her papa. She was big, too. Much larger than her mama. Her dark hair had streaks of gray on the sides and was pulled away from her face and wrapped in a knot on the back of her head. "Well, don't just stand there," the woman said sharply. "Your father'll help you take your things to your room and get you settled. We gave my son, Henry, your old room. He's eighteen years old and needs the larger room. We moved you to the room above the kitchen."

Mary was afraid to speak. What should she call this woman? She wasn't her mama. Mama died. Should she call her Mrs. Sutton? She couldn't call her Sarah. That wouldn't be proper.

"Yes, ma'am," Mary said softly under her breath as she followed Philip upstairs.

This wasn't exactly the homecoming that Mary was expecting. Her father's new wife was so cold, so sharp. And what happened to her room? Why did they give it to her son? Mary and Philip walked down the hallway. She saw Henry lying on the bed when they passed her old room. Henry glared at Mary and Philip when they passed. *Funny thing*, she thought, *lying around inside the house on a beautiful Sunday afternoon in July. Wouldn't he like to be outside?* That's where she would be, if she could. Philip opened the door to Mary's new room. He helped Mary unpack her things and put them way. The room was much smaller than her old room, but it didn't matter to her as long as she was home —home to stay.

Mary quickly fell into the routine of life at home again. Philip worked nights at the foundry. Every day Sarah prepared an early dinner before he left for work. Sometimes Henry was home for dinner, sometimes not. After dinner, Mary cleared the table. She had to use a step stool in order to reach the dish pan on the counter where she washed the dishes, dried them, and put them into the cupboard. She was allowed to play in the yard after dinner, but she always had to be in the house early. Sarah made her go to her room long before it got dark in the evening. Mary couldn't understand why. There was so much day-light yet to enjoy.

Sarah Sutton's mother, Emma, lived in a rented room in a house across the street. The white house with black shutters and trim had a steep, narrow staircase that led to the second story entry on the back-side of the house. Inside was a small pantry and kitchen. The bedroom had a single bed and a small window with white curtains overlooking the wooded backyard. The living room was good sized, much larger than the bedroom. There was a couch, a couple of chairs, and a large print rug on the dark hardwood floor. In the far corner of the room was a phonograph with a black morning-glory speaker on the top and a crank on the side of the dark wooden case. Metal cylinders were placed inside the wooden box. Several turns of the crank made a disc with a needle on the bottom go back and forth across the cylinder to produce music that blared from the cumbersome looking horn.

Mary liked to go to Emma's house. She was a plump old lady with a pleasing personality. Her bright white hair curled about her face and rosy red cheeks. She always wore a bib apron that she tied around her thick middle. Mary visited the old lady whenever she could. She called her Grandma.

"Hello, I'm here," Mary announced as she knocked on the wooden door of the old lady's house. "Hello." Mary could hear noise coming from inside of the house. The old lady came to the door, opened it and looked down at Mary.

"My goodness," Emma said. "I have a visitor. Would you like to come in?" Emma opened the door and Mary sneaked in under her arm.

"To what do I owe this pleasure today, Mary?"

"It's such a nice day outside today. I thought that I'd come for a visit. What are you doing?" The smell of fresh baked cookies rolled out of the warm kitchen. Mary was well aware of what Grandma had been up to.

"I baked molasses cookies today. Just took some from the oven. Would you like to test them for me? Let me know if they're any good?"

Mary nodded with excitement. Her new mama didn't bake cookies or much of anything for that matter. A cookie, especially a warm cookie, was an exceptional treat for her.

Emma pulled out a wooden chair from the table in the kitchen. Mary promptly sat on the chair as Emma handed her the warm cookie.

"Thank you, Grandma." Mary put the cookie to her nose. She closed her eyes and absorbed the smell of the spices. She nibbled the cookie.

"Mary, where's Lizzie? You didn't bring her with you today."

Mary was thoughtful for a moment. "Oh, she needed a nap. I left her at home on my bed."

"I'm sewing a new dress for Lizzie. I'm using fabric from one of my old aprons. Would you like to help me?" Mary popped the last of the cookie in her mouth and wiped her face clean with the back of her hand. "Come into the parlor." The old lady walked into the adjacent room. Mary followed, right at her heels. Emma lowered herself slowly into a wooden rocking chair. A large wicker sewing basket sat on the floor next to her chair. Emma lifted the lid of the basket, reached inside and pulled out a blue print dress that was held together with pins. "Maybe you can help me a bit, Mary. It's getting so hard for me to thread my sewing needles. I guess I don't see as well as I used to."

Mary sat cross-legged on the floor next to the old lady's rocker. She looked at Lizzie's new dress. The blue print fabric had a bit of white trim on the bottom of the skirt. Mary recognized it as an apron that Grandma had worn.

"What do you think?" Emma held the unfinished dress for Mary to see.

"It's beautiful. Lizzie will really like it."

"How about if I sew a bit while you're here. I only have a little sewing on the hem. You can take it home with you when you leave."

Mary sat patiently. Emma held the fine needle between her age-worn fingers. She carefully placed it in the white palm of Mary's tiny hand. Emma cut a piece of thread from a wooden spool. "Here." She handed Mary the thread. "You thread the needle for me, please."

Mary pinched the end of the thread between her fingers. She held the needle in the other and pushed the thread through the small eye of the needle before handing it back to the old lady. Emma sewed for a while and then handed the empty needle to Mary. Mary threaded it again, handed it back to Emma, and waited. "My, you do that quickly. I used to be able to thread my needles just like you until my eyesight got to be so bad."

Mary eyed the phonograph with the large horn in the corner. "Would you like to play some music, Mary? Do you remember how to put on the cylinder and turn the handle? Go ahead. We should listen to some music while we sew."

Mary carefully lifted the lid on the wooden phonograph case. She put the metal cylinder in place and then turned the handle on the side of the box several times. Scratchy music blared from the large, black horn.

Mary sat on the wooden floor at Emma's side, as she finished sewing the doll's dress. "Another job done," Emma said as she held the doll's dress for Mary to see.

"Thank you, Grandma. It's beautiful. Lizzie will really like it."

Emma handed Mary the dress. "There you are, my dear. You better be going home. Your mama'll be calling for you before long."

Mary stood up from the floor and walked with Emma toward the door. Emma stopped at a glass dish on the kitchen counter and picked out a piece of hard, yellow candy. She tucked the candy in Mary's dress pocket.

"You can save the candy for later." Emma smiled at Mary and patted her on the top of her head. "Thank you for coming to visit me, Mary." She held the door open, and Mary slipped out under her arm.

"Lizzie will really like her new dress. I'm going home right now to put it on her. Bye, Grandma." Mary held the doll's dress securely in one hand and gave a wave with the other. "I'll come back soon and help you thread your needles again." She ran down the old steps and across the street. "Bye, Grandma," she called again from the distance.

Mary ran to her bedroom. She couldn't wait for Lizzie to try on her new dress. She looked at her bed. Where was Lizzie? She wasn't on the bed. Mary was certain that she laid the doll down for a nap before she went to see Grandma. Mary stared in shock at the empty bed. Where could she have gone? Mary lifted the skirt of the quilt that covered the bed and look underneath—nothing there. She called out the doll's name in panic. She opened the closet door, but didn't find the doll either. Suddenly, Mary noticed Henry standing at the bedroom door with Lizzie in his hand. He was holding the doll by her hair high in the air. He gave Mary an evil look. "Is this what you're looking for? Looking for your stupid doll?"

Mary looked in horror as Lizzie dangled. "Give her to me," Mary cried. "Don't hurt her. Give her to me." Mary jumped to reach the doll, but Henry held the doll higher and higher. Why was Henry always so mean? She never did anything to bother him. She quickly learned that the best way to get along with him was to ignore him, which Mary did most of the time. Thankfully, Henry became bored rather quickly with his terrorism. He tossed the doll over Mary's head and onto the bed. Lizzie bounced and landed upside down near the foot of the bed.

"I don't want your stupid doll. You can have her." Henry walked down the hall. Mary could hear his evil-sounding laugh. She silently hoped that he was going away and would never return.

Mary rushed to the bed, picked up Lizzie, and brushed the doll's wild-looking hair with her hand. The doll rested in Mary's arms and closed its eyes. "I hope Henry didn't hurt you. I promise I'll never leave you alone with him again." Mary dried her tears with the back of her hand. She climbed on the bed. "Look, Lizzie, Grandma sewed you a new dress. Isn't it beautiful?" Mary undressed her doll and then put on her new dress. She rocked the doll gently and breathed a deep sigh of relief.

"Mary, Mary," Sarah called in a loud, harsh voice. "Come to the kitchen. Help me with dinner. Come now."

It was almost time for her papa to leave for work at the foundry. They always ate their evening meal just before he left for work. After dinner, Mary cleaned up the kitchen. Sarah usually sent her to her room for bed after the kitchen was cleaned. It was summertime. The days were long, and it was so warm outside. Why wasn't she allowed to go outside with the other children to play? She always got sent to bed so early, long before it ever got dark.

Mary missed her papa. She wished he was home after dinner. She liked to sit on his lap and listen to him talk or sing. Sometimes he'd read her a story. One time Philip brought out an old box with a blue wool uniform that he had worn when he was a soldier in the Civil War. He put on his uniform and told stories about going to war as a young man. Mary always listened carefully. She liked to learn about history.

After dinner Mary climbed the stairs to her room. She was lonely. Sarah wasn't anything like her mama. She never talked to her and certainly never played with her. She was a very cold and harsh woman who rarely smiled. The only time Sarah seemed to want Mary around was when there was work to be done.

Mary usually went to her room and played with Lizzie or her other toys until it was time to go to sleep. Sarah never came to check on her or help her get ready for bed, like her mama typically had. Sometimes Mary closed her eyes and tried to picture her mother's face. The image she saw in her mind was fuzzy—not as clear as it used to be. She squeezed her eyes tight and thought really hard, as far back as she could remember, but it didn't help make her mama's image appear any clearer. She never wanted to forget her mama, so she practiced remembering her image every night at bedtime.

Darkness was drawing near. Mary washed her hands and face in the basin on the counter in the pantry outside the kitchen. Sarah came in from the backyard and looked at Mary with surprise. "What are you doing down here? You're supposed to be in your room. I told you to get to bed long ago." Sarah grabbed Mary tight by one shoulder. She dug her fingers into Mary's arm. With her other hand she swatted Mary firmly on the butt. "Get going. Upstairs! Go!"

Mary quickly hopped down from the stool which tipped over and made a large bang on the wooden kitchen floor. With water dripping from her face and hands, Mary ran upstairs to the safe haven of her bedroom. She was afraid of what punishment might come if she didn't move quickly, as Sarah commanded.

The sun slipped past the horizon. It was a warm evening. A light breeze rustled the branches of the apple trees outside the window of Mary's bedroom. The sky was covered with stars, and the moon had come up among them. A wispy thin cloud passed over the face of the bright moon. Mary heard the back door of the house squeak and close shut. Mary moved quickly away from the front of the window so she wouldn't be seen. After a minute, she cautiously peeked around the edge of the window and peered into the yard. Sarah, wrapped in a dark shawl, was in the backyard. *What was she doing out there at this time of the night?* Mary wondered. Mary watched Sarah move across the yard and disappear quickly into the shadows of the night.

All of a sudden Mary realized that she was alone in the big dark house. Papa was at work and wouldn't be home until daybreak. Henry had been home at dinner, but she hadn't seen him since. Knowing her predicament, Mary grabbed Lizzie and moved to the corner of her room. She sat quietly on floor between the bed and the wall. She felt safe tucked into the corner out of view. She was terrified to be alone. The old house creaked and made haunting noises in the wind. Peculiar noises that she never heard during the daytime echoed loud in the quiet of the night.

A long time passed. Mary was growing tired, so she pulled back the covers on her bed and slid inside. She rested her head on the pillow and pulled Lizzie close to her little body. She was lying there sleepless for a while when she heard a man's voice. Was it her papa? Had papa come home? The man's voice came from the backyard. Excited to see her papa, Mary hopped out of bed and ran to the window. She looked outside and realized that the voice she heard wasn't her papa's. Rather, there was a strange man in the backyard talking to Sarah. Mary quickly backed away from the window and slid up tight against the wall. She held her breath. Her heart pounded hard in her tiny chest. She didn't want Sarah or the strange man to see her. After a couple minutes Mary mustered a bit of courage and quickly she glanced into the backyard again. Sarah stood with her back to the window. Mary could see Sarah's long dark hair draped on her back and shoulders. Sarah looked so different—she usually wore her hair tied neatly on the back of her head in a bun. The strange man walked hurriedly across the backyard and vanished into the shadows. Frightened and disconcerted by what she saw, Mary jumped back into her bed. She pulled the covers under her chin and closed her eyes and pretended that she was asleep. She didn't want Sarah to know what she had just seen.

Mary went about the business of the next day and hardly spoke a word to Sarah. She was afraid to be near Sarah. Mary was afraid of what Sarah might do to her if she learned that Mary had seen her in the backyard with a strange man. After dinner that night Philip went to work at the foundry. As usual, Mary helped clean the kitchen and was sent off to her bedroom early, well before dark. She sat on her bed and played with Lizzie. All of a sudden, a strange noise came from under her bed. Mary sat motionless and held her breath. Perhaps she imagined the noise. She sat for a long time without moving, then she heard the noise again. It sounded like a man moaning. Maybe it was the strange man that she had seen in the backyard. Maybe he saw her looking out the window and wanted to be sure that she didn't tell anyone what she had seen. Maybe he came to get her in the night.

Mary was terrified. Her body started to shake. Suddenly, a large hand reached out from under the bed. The large hand grabbed at the top of the bed like it was trying to snatch her. Mary slid quickly to the other side of the bed. Another hand grabbed at her from the other side of the bed. She cried out in terror. She wanted to run from the room, but the hands reached up as she shifted from side to side in the bed. The man under the bed moaned and groaned. "I'm going to get you, Mary." The man's voice droned. "I'm going to throw you off the bridge and into the river."

A rustling and banging noise came from under the bed. The bed moved. The man was trying to get out. She needed to run—run quickly. Just then Henry emerged. He looked into Mary's terrified eyes swollen with tears. He raised his arms high in the air. In a loud voice he yelled, "Boo! Scared ya'. Scared ya'. You fraidy cat." Henry put his face close to Mary's. She sat motionless, and her eyes were big. She was afraid to breathe. Henry laughed loudly, holding his stomach and walked from the room.

Mary wasn't sure what to do. Her hands were sweaty. She took short, deep breaths. Her body was shaking all over. She wanted to tell Sarah, but was enormously frightened to leave her room. What if Henry was waiting for her outside her room? What if that strange man that she had seen in the backyard had come back? She wanted her papa. It would be morning before he'd come home, however. She couldn't wait that long. She thought about Grandma in her apartment across the street. It would be impossible for her to sneak out of the house without Sarah seeing her.

Mary crawled under the covers of her bed, too terrified to put her feet on the floor and walk to her bureau to get her night dress. She knew that Henry had left the room, but she was terrified. Mary pulled the covers over her head and slid down to the foot of the bed. She fell asleep.

Daylight was streaming in her bedroom window when Mary woke. She could hear her papa's and Sarah's voices coming through the register in the floor of her room that led to the kitchen. They were talking very loudly, much louder that usual. Sarah's voice was sharp. Her sentences short. She could hear her papa's quiet voice reply. Mary couldn't make out what they were saying, although it sounded like they were arguing. Sarah was making breakfast. The smell of coffee drifted into Mary's room.

Mary started to get out of her bed. Suddenly she remembered the horror of the night before and quickly pulled her legs back up onto the mattress. She lay on her stomach and lowered her head slowly over the edge of the bed. Cautiously, she pulled up the sheets and looked under the bed. It was empty. She breathed a heavy sigh of relief when she discovered that no one was under her bed. Mary walked across the room to her bureau and then realized she had slept all night in her dress. She brushed the wrinkles out of her dress, put on her socks and shoes, and walked to the kitchen. She wanted to tell her papa what happened during the night but was fearful to say anything in front of Sarah. It would have to wait for another time. Should she tell Papa about the man in the backyard, too? That might have to wait for another time as well. Her biggest problem right now was Sarah's son, Henry, and his frequent acts of terror against her.

Mary saw Philip sitting silently at the table when she walked into the kitchen. Sarah turned quickly and worked at the kitchen counter. They stopped talking when Mary walked into the room. They must have been talking about something that they didn't want her to hear.

Mary pulled up a chair and sat at the table. She dished eggs from the bowl on the table and put them on her plate. Papa didn't even look her way. Sarah poured Mary a cup of milk and placed it hard in the table in front of her. Milk spilled onto the table.

"When you're done with breakfast I want you to clean the kitchen," Sarah barked. "Then you can come outside and help me with the laundry."

Philip stood up from the table. Looking at the floor as he walked, he silently left the room. He didn't even acknowledge Mary.

Their lives certainly had taken a sad turn from the days when Mary's mama was alive. They were such a happy family in a loving home. She secretly wished that it could be that way again. Mary watched her papa's tired body as he shuffled from the room and left the house.

Philip came home late in the day, almost at the time for him to go to work at the foundry. Mary didn't know where he had been all day. "Papa, Papa," Mary said in a whisper of a voice. She tugged at the leg of his trousers as she walked close to his side. She looked around to be sure that no one was watching. "Papa, I'm scared. I'm scared to be here at night when you go to work. Don't go to work tonight, please, please don't go." Mary pleaded with her father. He gazed at Mary.

"Mary, I have to go to work. There's nothing for you to be afraid of. Nothing's going to happen to you when I'm at work."

"But, Papa, Henry scares me. Sometimes when you're gone he goes under my bed. He makes strange noises. He grabs at me when I'm sitting on my bed. I'm afraid he's going to be under my bed when I go up to bed tonight."

"Mary, I'll look under your bed before I go to work tonight. Let's go upstairs right now and look. I'm sure he's not there. No one's under your bed."

"No, he's not there now, but he will be after you go to work. Sometimes he takes Lizzie away from me. He holds my doll by her hair over my head. I jump, but I can't reach her. Please make him stop."

Philip walked into Mary's room. He lifted the quilt and looked under the bed. He held the covers up so that Mary could look. "See, there's no one under your bed." Mary peeked under her bed. It was empty just as her father had said. But just wait, Mary knew that he would come back again.

"Mary, I need to go to work. I'll talk to Henry the next time I see him. I'll ask him not to bother you anymore. Now, go help Sarah with dinner. You know she'll get angry with you if you're not there to help in the kitchen. Go." Philip walked away and left Mary standing alone at the edge of her bed.

After dinner that night Sarah sent Mary to bed. It was early in the evening, as usual. As night drew near, Mary heard a man's voice in the backyard. Mary slipped off the bed and walked to the window. She put her back up to the wall so she wouldn't be seen. She stood very still.

Quickly, she sneaked a peek into the backyard that was surrounded by a wall of dark gray trees of assorted sizes. There was no wind and nothing stirred their leafless branches. The man she had seen so many times before had returned. She waited. The door to the house squeaked. She heard Sarah's voice and then the man's as they entered the house.

Terrified, Mary ran and hid under her bed. If the man came to her room he'd never be able to see her. She clenched Lizzie tight while she looked across the wood floor, through the doorway and into the hall outside her room. She lay motionless under her bed on the hardwood floor. She was scared to move a muscle. She was even too frightened to breathe.

Mary could hear quiet voices coming up through the metal register in the floor of her room. The man from the backyard was in the kitchen with Sarah. Their voices were muffled, so she couldn't make out what they were saying. Just then, Mary realized if she moved a little closer to the head of the bed she could put her ear on the register. She could hear what they were saying.

She slid her body across the floor carefully. She didn't want to make any noise or surely they'd hear. Mary turned her head and laid her ear on the opening in the floor. Not only could she hear better, but she could see all the way clear down to the kitchen. Sarah stood with her back at the counter. A man with a liquor bottle stood facing Sarah. He whispered something. Mary couldn't make out what he said.

"No, don't worry. He's not home. He won't be home for several hours," Mary heard Sarah say. The man whispered again in a soft, deep voice. Sarah replied, "She's in bed. I sent her there a long time ago. She's asleep by now."

Sarah was talking about her. She wasn't in bed, much less asleep. Mary knew that she had to be very still and not make any noise. If Sarah knew she was watching and listening there would be trouble. For sure Sarah would take her into the yard and use the switch on her as she had before when Mary didn't behave or do what she was asked.

The man reached his hand to Sarah's head and touched her hair in the knot at the back of her head. Her dark hair fell gently onto her

101

shoulders. The man ran both of his hands through Sarah's hair, drew her close, and kissed her on the lips. Sarah smiled and giggled quietly. Why was this strange man kissing her father's wife? That wasn't right. He shouldn't even be in the house. What would Papa do if he knew?

Mary turned her head and lay on her back. She stared at the bottom side of her bed. She didn't want to see anymore. It hurt her to think that Sarah had a boyfriend coming to the house while her father was at work. It wasn't right. Papa wouldn't be happy if he knew what was going on. She was afraid to tell him however because she was afraid it would lead to another argument between him and Sarah. Their arguments had grown more frequent recently.

Mary slid out from under the bed. She pulled back the quilt that covered her bed and crawled underneath. "Lizzie, I'm scared," Mary whispered in the doll's small ear. "What should I do? Papa'll get so angry if I tell him about the strange man I saw in the kitchen with Sarah." She lay still on her back and fell fast asleep with Lizzie snuggled in her arms.

ೞ 10 ೲ

MARY COULD HARDLY WAIT UNTIL SCHOOL started again. She missed her classmates and her teacher, Miss Hastings. She also longed to learn how to read and write. Reading was her favorite subject. Most of all, she welcomed the school year so that she didn't have to spend her days at home with Sarah.

Mary looked forward to seeing her father for a short while every day after school. He left for work at the foundry immediately after dinner. She always had the opportunity to tell him what she learned at school. He never said too much, although he seemed proud of her in his own quiet way.

Sometimes, while Mary cleaned up after the meal, she could hear her father and Sarah talking in the parlor. Sarah's voice always was harsh. She made quick, short comments to her father. Rarely, however, could she hear her father's quiet reply. Mary couldn't understand what her father had done to make her so angry all the time. He was a good man who provided his family. There was always good food on the table.

The only time Mary ever saw Sarah smile was when the strange man came for a visit. He came frequently, about the same time almost every day, not long after Philip left for the foundry. The man stayed until after Mary went to sleep. He always came through the back door. One night, it was very cold and windy outside. It had rained during the day, which had turned to big flakes of snow during the evening. The man arrived at the usual time. He wore a winter coat, hat, and gloves. Mary heard Sarah take his coat and ask him to stand by the stove to warm up. Mary really didn't care to hear what was happening in the kitchen because she knew it would hurt her father so much if he ever found out. As usual, Mary pulled the covers over her head and slipped off to sleep.

The next day, after school, as always, Mary went to the well, lowered the wooden bucket, and filled it with water. She carried the bucket of water into the house. On her way, she saw a dark piece of cloth covered by a light coat of freshly fallen snow. Mary put down the bucket of water, bent over, and dusted off the cloth. It was a man's glove. She picked it up and held it in her hand. Just then, Philip came out of the house.

"Mary, hurry up and get in the house. You're going to freeze to death out there. Hurry on. Bring the bucket inside." Philip noticed the glove in her hand and walked into the yard. "Mary, I told you to hurry on." He looked at the glove. "What's that you have in your hand? Where did you get that glove? Is that one of mine?" Mary was sure she knew who the glove belonged to, but wasn't sure what she should say. She stood silent, staring at the man's glove. Philip took the glove from Mary. It didn't look like any that he owned.

"Where did you find this?"

Mary pointed to the ground where she had uncovered the glove. "Right here, Papa."

Philip could see the bare grass where the glove had lain.

"Looks like someone dropped it here. Humpf, I wonder who it belongs to."

Philip picked up Mary's bucket of water with one hand and held the glove in the other. Mary couldn't stay quiet any longer. She blurted, "It belongs to the man who comes to visit at night."

Philip stopped short in his tracks. He turned around quickly and glared at Mary. She had never seen that shocked look on her father's face. Mary didn't move. She didn't notice the cold wind blowing against her fair skin. Her cheeks were bright pink.

"What man who comes at night?"

Mary knew that it was too late to take back her words. She was afraid to speak in fear of what her father's reaction might be.

"Mary, I asked you a question. Answer me! I said, what man who comes at night?"

Mary's lips trembled in fear, not from the cold. She immediately regretted the comment that she made about the man. Then a moment later she thought that perhaps it was a good thing, after all Philip would probably learn about the man sooner or later. She was hoping, though, that it wouldn't have come from her because she didn't want to hurt her papa. Tears streamed down her frosty cheeks.

"Oh, Papa. There's a man who comes to visit Sarah sometimes at night. He came many times during the summer. He hasn't been here for quite a while, but he returned last night. I saw him from my bedroom window when he came to the house. He was wearing a coat and gloves. That's one of his gloves. He must have dropped it when he left."

"Who is this man? Do you know him? Do you recognize him?"

Mary shook her head.

"Where were you when the man came to visit?"

"I stay in my room, Papa. I always do. I see the man come to the back door, and then I can hear him and Sarah talk in the kitchen through the register in the floor of my room. Sometimes I can see them, too, but most of the time, at least in the summer, they'd leave the house together and don't come back until after I went to sleep."

Philip stood in shock as he looked at Mary. He couldn't believe what he was hearing. "Mary, get in the house and go to your room. Now!"

"Papa, don't be mad at me. I'm sorry," she cried. "I didn't do anything wrong."

"Go now!" Philip commanded.

"I was going to tell you before, but I was afraid that you would get mad at me. I was afraid of what might happen. I was afraid you would take me back to the country, and I wouldn't be able to live with you anymore."

Mary ran into the house and up the wooden stairs to her bedroom. She passed Sarah, who was standing at the counter in the kitchen. Sarah turned and gave Mary a harsh look as she fled past. Philip picked up the bucket of water as he tucked the soiled, wet man's glove into his pocket. He marched into the kitchen and slammed the door so hard behind him that the dishes rattled in the cupboard. Philip set the water bucket on the counter with such authority that its contents sloshed over the sides and onto the floor. He glared at Sarah as he passed her.

"So what's wrong with the little brat this time? Whining again about having to fetch the water?"

Philip didn't acknowledge Sarah's question as he quickly walked up the stairs to Mary's room. The pounding of his feet on the wooden steps echoed through the house.

Mary was lying face down on her bed. Philip entered the room, sat on the edge of the bed, and touched the back of Mary's head. She rolled over and faced Philip. Her face was red and bits of her yellow hair were plastered to her face by her tears. Philip brushed the wet hair from her round face and dried her tears with the sleeve of his plaid work shirt. "Mary, I'm not angry at you for telling me about the man. You did the right thing by telling me."

"Oh, Papa. I was so scared some nights when she'd leave with the man. She'd leave me alone at night, all alone in the dark. Sometimes Henry would sneak into my room and scare me. He'd crawl under my bed and make strange growling noises. Sometimes he'd grab at me from under my bed. Lizzie and I had to sit in the middle of the bed so he wouldn't get us. I don't like Henry, Papa. He scares me too much."

"Mary, don't worry about Henry. I'll talk with Sarah about him. Don't worry. He won't be scaring you anymore. As for the man, he won't be coming to the house at night anymore either. I promise. I promise. I'll take care of that, too."

Mary could see the fingers of the man's glove sticking out of Philip's pocket. "Are you going to see the man, Papa? Will you tell him not to come over anymore at night?"

"Don't worry, Mary. I'll take care of it. The man'll never come back. He'll never set foot in this house again." Philip left the room. Mary could hear his heavy work boots on the wooden stairs. She sat up on the bed, straightened her clothes, and brushed her hair with her fingers.

"Well, did you punish the little brat?" Sarah asked. "Did you tell her not to come down for dinner? Might be good for her to be without dinner once and a while. Maybe she'd start to learn. She whines far too much about having to do the smallest chores, Philip. I'm tired of listening to her. I think a good whipping once and a while would do her some good. Make her straighten up."

Mary sat straight up on her bed. Her body stiffened. "Oh, please, no Papa. Don't let Sarah hit me again. I'll try harder. I promise to be good," Mary whispered to herself.

Mary witnessed Sarah's violent temper several times in the past. She remembered the time that she was helping Sarah hang the wash in the backyard. Mary took each piece of wet clothing from the laundry basket and handed it to Sarah so she could hang it on the clothesline. Accidentally Mary dropped a piece of laundry on the ground. Sarah lost her temper and grabbed Mary by the arm. Sarah shook Mary so hard that she thought her arm was going to fall off. Then, Sarah picked up a willowy tree branch from the ground and hit Mary several times across the backside as she screamed at her.

Mary continued to listen to their conversation. "Sarah, stop it! Mary wasn't complaining about the water. It seems Henry likes to go into her room at night and scare the living daylights out of her. He crawls under her bed. Where were you when he did these things? How come you don't tell him to keep away from her?"

"Oh, Henry's not doing any such thing. Philip. She's making up stories again. You know that child has a wild imagination. Probably just making up a story to get more attention."

"Sounds just like something Henry would do, Sarah. He's always picking on her. He needs to grow up and act his age. I'm going to talk with Henry. It's time for him to get out on his own. Find some work. Find another place to live. I don't know why he's living here anyway. I think he's the one that could use a good whipping. That boy needs someone to straighten him up."

Philip's loud, angry voice frightened Mary. She never heard him use that tone of voice with her mother. He raised his voice at Sarah again and again. Mary didn't like their arguments, especially when Sarah yelled back at her father. Their loud voices echoed through the house.

Mary remembered the way that it used to be, the way it was when her mother was alive. Why did her mother have to die? Why couldn't it be that way again? Why did she leave her and Papa? Mary closed her eyes and tried to imagine her mother's face, but her image was faint and obscure. It was getting harder and harder to remember her likeness. Oh, how she longed to sit on her mother's lap and feel her arms wrapped securely about her. Mary remembered her mother's sweet smell—like a fresh bouquet of flowers from the garden.

Suddenly, a loud bang came from the kitchen. It was the sound of Philip's fist hitting the kitchen table. "Mary's my daughter! She's not going anywhere."

Mary had never heard her father so angry. Her eyes swelled with tears, and she shook with fear. "Please don't fight. Please don't yell." Mary grabbed the pillow from her bed and squeezed it tightly over her ears. It only muffled their voices.

"That's the last I want to hear talk of sending Mary away. She's part of our family. That's the last of it."

A deadly quiet came from the kitchen. The yelling stopped. Mary was afraid to take a breath. "Please stay quiet. Please don't start yelling again."

"Mary," her father shouted. "Come and eat. It's time for dinner. It's getting late, and I need to go to work."

Gingerly, Mary put one foot on the floor, then the other. She was afraid to go to the kitchen, but was more afraid if she didn't go. Apprehensively she made her way down the hall and tip-toed down the stairs very slowly. Mary peered around the corner and peeked into the kitchen when she reached the final stair. Philip was seated at the table with his back toward her. Steam billowed from a dish of potatoes that Sarah carried to the table. Sarah paused and glared at Mary while she passed.

"Wash your hands and then sit and eat." Those were the only words spoken during the entire meal. Philip finished his meal and then quietly put on his heavy coat and hat. He looked back at Mary and Sarah, who were sitting at the table. "I'm going to be late for work before long." He walked out of the house and closed the door tightly behind him.

Mary and Sarah sat in silence at the table. Mary was much too frightened to speak.

"Clear the table, Mary. Do the dishes and then get to bed," were Sarah's only words to her that evening.

Mary took the apron from the hook on the wall in the corner and slipped it over her head. She wrapped the ties of the apron around her and made them into a loose bow. Mary cleared the table while water for washing dishes warmed on the stove. She washed each dish and then rinsed it in another dishpan. She worked quickly but carefully. She couldn't imagine the horror if she broke a plate or a cup. She couldn't wait to finish her chores so she could get away from Sarah. This was one night when she couldn't wait to get to her bedroom. She was much too frightened to spend any more time with Sarah than she needed to.

Sarah went into the bedroom and shut the door. Philip and Sarah's bedroom was opposite the hall from the kitchen. Mary dried the dishes with a large white flour-sack towel. She opened the cupboards and put the dishes where they belonged. Carefully, she poured the dirty water from the dish pan through the hole in the counter and into the slop pail below. When all the dishes were done, Mary hung the dish-towel near the stove to dry. She opened the curtain on the cupboard and looked at the slop pail. It was almost full. Sarah or Papa would have to empty that bucket another time. It was much too large for her to carry. Mary surveyed the kitchen to be sure that she hadn't missed anything. She remembered the time that she forgot to wash the fry pan. Sarah became so angry at her, she grabbed the broom from the corner and hit Mary sharply across her wrists. She never wanted that to happen again.

Mary untied her apron, slipped it off and then hung it on the hook where she kept it. It was a very clear evening, and it was starting to get dark outside. A gentle wind blew lightly from the west. She could hear an owl *woo*ing in the distance. If she listened carefully, she could hear noise from the foundry where her father worked. It was time for bed.

Mary passed Sarah at the doorway to her bedroom as she left the kitchen. Sarah seemed surprised to see her and grumbled at Mary. "Did you finish in the kitchen?" Sarah didn't wait for Mary to reply. "Go to your room. Get to bed."

Sarah had removed her house dress and apron that she wore when they ate dinner. She was wearing a dark-blue dress that opened at the neck. It had a lacy, white collar and buttons all the way down the front. Sarah usually wore this dress only for good like when they went to church. Mary had never seen her wear it on a week night. Then Mary noticed the sweet smell of Sarah's perfume. "Did you hear me, you little brat? I told you to get to your room, now. Go, now!" Sarah grabbed Mary and pinched her shoulder hard, and swatted Mary firmly on the butt. "You're sure are a nosey little thing. Get upstairs. Now!"

Sarah loosened her tight grip on Mary's shoulder. Realizing her freedom, Mary ran up the stairs as quickly as she could. She went to her room and promptly closed the door behind her. Mary was becoming familiar with Sarah's sneaky ways. Sarah's visitor couldn't return to the house since Mary had found the man's glove in the backyard and given it to Philip. It was obvious that Philip had become suspicious.

About half an hour after Mary went to her room, she heard the back door of the house shut. Mary got out of bed, went to the window, and pulled back the white curtain. The moon beamed in the dark sky and cast eerie shadows in the backyard. Mary saw Sarah walk across the yard and slip into the darkness. Once again she was alone in the big old house. Creaking in the house sounded so much louder when she knew that she was alone. Henry had been gone for several days so he shouldn't be there to frighten her. She overheard him telling Sarah that he heard there was work in St. Paul at one of the mills. She hoped he had found a job there and wouldn't return.

Mary crawled back into bed, grabbed Lizzie, and held her tight. Lizzie offered her the comfort she needed to fall asleep. Mary pulled the covers over her head and lay very still. If someone came into her room, maybe they wouldn't notice her. She fell asleep. Although she didn't know exactly when, maybe around midnight, a noise from the kitchen awoke Mary. She didn't get up right away because she was scared of who might be in the house with her.

"Shhh! Shhh! Be quiet. You have to be quiet," Sarah whispered in a low voice. "Philip's little girl is upstairs, asleep in her room. We can't wake her."

Mary stirred in her bed. She pulled the covers from over her head and tucked them under her chin. She opened her eyes and saw the moonshine coming over the top of the curtain that covered her bedroom window. She found Lizzie and pulled her close. Suddenly, she heard a man's voice, "I brought a bottle from the saloon. I'll pour you another drink. Where are the glasses?"

Mary's body froze. There was a man in the house, and it wasn't Papa. The voice came from the kitchen.

"We have to be quiet, Warren," Sarah said in a loud whisper. "We can't wake her. Let's go into the parlor. It's not so close to her room. She can't hear anything from the front side of the house."

Mary heard the heavy footsteps of a man that she was certain wasn't her father. Suddenly there was a loud noise followed by laughter. The man had stumbled on the rug in the hall at the doorway to the parlor and landed on the floor with a loud thud. Sarah and the man both laughed loudly. "Warren, give me the bottle. I'm glad it didn't break. Get up. Let's go in here. You have to be quiet, though. We don't want to wake her." Little did Sarah know that Mary lay awake in her bed listening to every word. Sarah must have put on her good blue dress so she could go to the saloon in town. So that's where she went when she left the house earlier. Mary could still hear the man's voice and Sarah's laughter, although she couldn't make out what they were saying. The noise from the parlor stopped, and Mary fell fast asleep.

෩ 11 ඥ

G ET OUT! GET OUT OF MY HOUSE! Now!" Mary awoke to her father's angry voice coming from the parlor. Philip had come home from work about an hour earlier than the time that he usually arrived. When he walked in the house he saw Sarah and Warren on the sofa in the parlor. Dirty drink glasses and an empty liquor bottle littered the room, and the smell of stale alcohol permeated the air. Sarah and Warren both had had too much to drink and had fallen asleep. Philip grabbed Warren by the shoulder, pulled him off the sofa, and threw him to the floor. Warren's head hit hard on the wood floor while his legs knocked over half empty drink glasses. Glass shattered everywhere.

"Philip, Philip. Stop!" Sarah screamed.

Philip picked Warren up by his clothing and threw him hard against the wall. He hit a small wooden end table near the window. The beautiful colored glass lamp on the table crashed to the floor and broke into a thousand tiny fragments. Philip grabbed Warren tightly at the neck and threw him up hard against the wall again. He made a fist and struck Warren in the face. A steady stream of bright red blood poured from Warren's nose. Philip struck Warren again and again. Sarah tried to restrain Philip, but his strong arms moved quickly. She couldn't get near Philip without risking being struck herself. Finally, when Warren's body went limp, Philip let him go, and Warren slid down the wall and onto the floor with a loud thud. His left eye was bruised and swelling. Blood flowed from several deep cuts in his face. Sarah watched in horror.

Philip turned to Sarah. His face was bright red, and he had a look of rage on his face like he'd been possessed by a demon. "So is this the man that's been coming to the house while I'm at work? I finally caught you, Sarah. I finally caught you."

"He's never been at the house before, Philip. I met him at the saloon. He came back to the house with me. We had a couple drinks and fell asleep on the sofa. He's never been here before."

"You're lying, Sarah. Don't lie to me. I know he's been here."

Warren stirred on the floor. He wiped the dripping blood from his nose and then wrapped his arms around himself. Broken glass crunched under Philip's shoes as he moved closer to Sarah.

"If this man hasn't been here before, then who was, Sarah? I know you've had other visitors. How many men have you been keeping? Is there a different man that comes to see you every night while I'm at work?"

Sarah's blue dress was twisted on her body. The knot of hair on top of her head had come undone. She brushed the hair from her eyes. She wondered how Philip knew that she had been unfaithful. How had he learned about her male visitors? She was always careful to clean up after they left. Maybe Mary had heard or seen something and told her father. *Leave it to that little brat to tell on her*, Sarah thought. *That no good child.*

Warren gingerly rose to his knees and crawled slowly across the parlor floor. He held his hand to his stomach. Philip turned and swiftly planted his heavy work boot firmly into Warren's ribs. Warren collapsed to the floor again and rolled painfully from side to side.

"Philip, please don't strike him again. Leave him alone," Sarah begged as she tugged at the sleeve of Philip's heavy coat. Sarah wiped away the tears that streamed down her cheeks.

114

"So, I suppose you're going to tell me that you're sorry. I know you've had men come to the house before. It's too late Sarah. You can't take it back. What's done is done."

Sarah moved closer to Philip. "I'm sorry. I didn't mean for it to happen. It's been so hard for me since I moved to Owatonna."

"I don't need to hear your feeble excuses. I've provided for you and your son, and this is what you do?"

Warren tried to get to his feet, but fell back to the floor. Philip wasn't sure if Warren was unable to get up because he was injured or intoxicated. Warren started to crawl again, slowly. Philip and Sarah watched him. When Warren reached the door, he grabbed the door knob and used it to pull himself up. Hunched over and grabbing his sides, he opened the door and staggered out of the house.

"Don't you ever set foot in this house again, you sorry good-for-nothing," Philip yelled at Warren as he left the house. "You'll pay a hefty price if you do. This is just a sample of the beating that you'll get if I ever see you again."

Sarah moved to the door and closed it behind him. She watched as Warren painfully wobbled away.

"I know you're lying, Sarah. I know there have been other men." Philip reached deep into his coat pocket. He pulled out the man's glove that Mary had found in the backyard. "Who does this belong to?" Philip asked as he shook the glove in Sarah's face. "Tell me. Another one of your many suitors?"

Sarah looked in disbelief and stumbled on her words, "I . . . I don't know. Where did you get that glove?" She wiped the end of her nose with the back of her hand.

"Mary found it in the backyard a few weeks ago."

"I should have known. That child has never liked me. She's had it in for me ever since you brought her back home, Philip."

"Sarah, it's not Mary's fault that one of your boyfriends lost his glove in the backyard. She didn't do anything wrong. I saw her pick the glove off the ground and took it from her."

"Philip, I haven't been happy ever since Mary came to live with us. I never wanted to have another child. I raised Henry alone after my husband died. It was difficult. Much harder than I ever thought. I was looking forward to Henry moving out and finally getting out on his own. I'm too old and tired to raise a child again, especially someone else's child, and an orphan besides. Mary has done whatever she could to make my life miserable."

Philip and Sarah turned when they heard a noise from the top of the staircase. Mary, dressed in her night dress, was standing on the top stair. Lizzie dangled in her hand. Her face was sad and tears rolled down her cheeks.

"How long have you been standing there, Mary? What did you hear?" Philip asked.

Mary didn't answer. She ran into her room and closed the door tightly behind her.

"Philip, we have to do something about her. I don't want to raise another child. Either she goes or I go," Sarah said with certainty.

Philip couldn't believe what he had just heard. He wasn't expecting such a firm ultimatum.

"Philip, you heard me. It's her or me. You have to admit that it's been hard on you, too, since she came back. It'll be several more years before she's ready to move out on her own, and I'm too old and tired to raise another child. What man can raise a daughter alone? You tried it before after Josie died, and you couldn't do it by yourself. What makes you think that you could raise her alone now?"

Hearing Josie's name brought back memories to Philip. They had had such a wonderful life together. He and Mary and Josie were a happy family. Philip remembered the day that they traveled to the church home and adopted Mary. Josie beamed when the nun placed the tiny baby in her arms. She was so happy to have a child. She was the perfect wife and mother. His life had taken a terrible turn.

"What do you want me to do, Sarah? Take Mary back out in the country to the Clausens again? They already have one child, Helen

Lucille. Mrs. Clausen's an invalid. She's in a wheelchair. It's hard enough for her as is. I don't think she wants a second child to care for."

"Mary could be a big help to Mrs. Clausen. Mary's older and can do more chores around the house. I'm sure Mrs. Clausen would appreciate having someone to help her. Also, Mary could have a sister. Might be good for her to have another child in the family."

"Sarah, I'm not asking the Clausens again. It's not right. Go get yourself cleaned up. It's time for breakfast, and Mary needs to get ready for school. We'll talk more after she leaves."

Sarah changed into her house dress and fixed her hair into the bun on top of her head. She put on an apron and wrapped the ties around her thick waist as she walked up the stairs to Mary's room. Sarah knocked hard on the door and opened it. "Get dressed for school, Mary, and come down for breakfast. Hurry. You don't have much time. It's getting late."

Philip opened the door to the stove and built up the fire. He tended the fire in the stove in the parlor too. It was cold outside, a typical early March day in Minnesota. A strong north wind sent whirlpools of snow swirling through the air. He stared blankly out the window while he thought about the difficult decision he had to make.

"Philip, Philip," Sarah barked. "Philip, did you hear me. Breakfast is ready." Philip stared at the dreadful mess in the parlor. The beautiful hand-painted glass lamp he had given Josie one year for Christmas was shattered in a thousand pieces on the parlor floor. Drinking glasses were overturned and their contents poured out. A half-empty liquor bottle lay tipped on its side. What a shattered mess. The sickening site reminded him of the fragments of his life.

Sarah set an earthenware bowl of fluffy yellow scrambled eggs on the table. She sliced bread, put it on a plate, and brought it to the table. Neither Mary nor Philip looked up. Philip wondered how much of the fight Mary had heard. He wondered if she had heard their conversation after Warren had left. He hoped that she hadn't but was fearful that she had.

117

Philip looked sadly at Mary while she ate. Poor child, Philip thought, she really deserved to have a loving family. She adjusted so well after Josie's death. And even the year she spent with the Clausens didn't seem to have an effect on her. He thought that she would finally be able to have a normal family life with him and Sarah, but sometimes things just don't work out like one hopes.

Mary finished her breakfast, picked up her dishes and took them to the dish pan on the counter. Normally, it was her job to wash the dishes before she went to school. There was no time this morning. She needed to leave soon, or she would be late for school. Mary was afraid that she would anger Sarah if she asked permission to skip her morning chores.

"Mary, it's time for you to leave for school. Dress warm. It's cold outside, and the wind's blowing strong." Mary stood still in amazement. Sarah never let her go to school before doing chores. Mary quickly put on her blue-and-black plaid winter coat and sat on the kitchen floor while she pulled on her heavy winter boots. Philip took Mary's knit hat from the shelf, put it on her head, and pulled it securely over her ears. "Walk quickly, Mary. You'll stay warmer," Philip told her. "Hurry on. You don't want to be late."

Mary slipped on her woolen mittens and rushed out the door. Philip closed the door tightly after Mary and watched her walk hurriedly towards the brick schoolhouse and out of his sight.

Marjorie Peterson, age ninety-one.

"The Green, Green Grass of Home," by Ann Zemke.

Above: Train depot: Mary Sutton was selected from the orphan train by Peter and Grace Lind, Bertha, Minnesota, on November 20, 1906. Below left: Cottage No. 5. Mary Sutton lived in Cottage No. 5 in the State School Orphanage, Owatonna, Minnesota. The tree to the left of the square symbolizes that George Peterson often made his living by chopping wood and logging. Below right: Wedding rings: George and Marjorie Peterson were married sixty-four years.

At left: Twenty colored fabrics surround the hearts–one for each grandchild. Twenty-five colored hearts–one for each great-grandchild. Three white hearts–one for each great-great-grandchild.

Below left: Red, White, and Blue: Marjorie's favorite holidays were Memorial Day and the Fourth of July.

Right: Church: Marjorie was a very active member of the Ladies Aid Group of the Long Prairie United Methodist Church.

359
Lap robes

Top: Pillowcase: Overnight guests always slept on a hand-embroidered pillow-case at Marjorie's house. Bottom: Old-fashioned Sewing Machine: In her later years, Marjorie sewed three hundred fifty-nine lap robes (lap quilts) that she donated to the veterans' home.

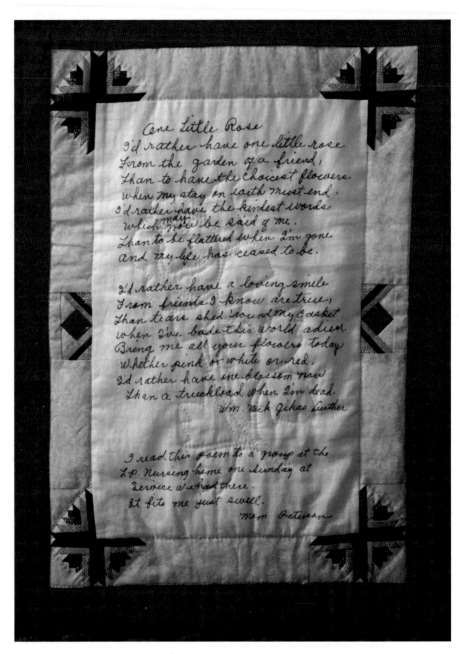

One Little Rose: Marjorie's favorite poem.

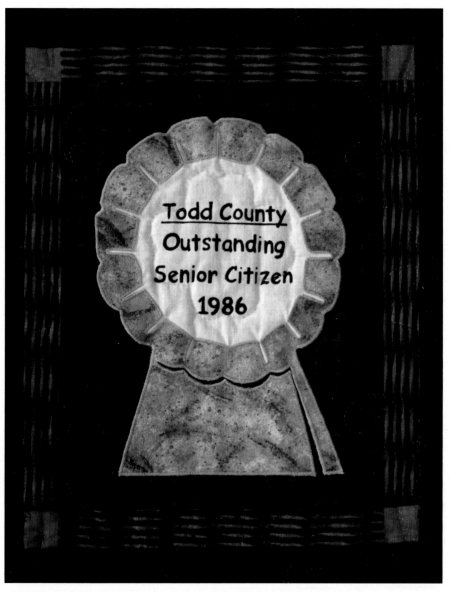

Award: Marjorie was named as Todd County's Outstanding Senior Citizen in 1986 at the age of eighty-eight.

Gardener: Marjorie often sold her garden produce to the Long Prairie High School across the street. The charm bracelet on her wrist has one charm for each of her grandchildren.

ଚ 12 ର

MARY PULLED BACK THE WHITE LACE CURTAIN that covered her bedroom window. The day was kissed with bright early morning sunshine. She closed her eyes quickly, and then opened them again slowly as they adjusted to the bright light. It was mid-March, and spring had come early this year. The only snow remaining was in the large banks that Philip had shoveled throughout the winter. Even these were dwindling fast. Small streams of water trickled from the snow piles into the yard. Slices of new green grass peeked out throughout the yard. Mary pulled up her window. The breeze against her face felt fresh and damp. A robin with its beak full of straw perched on the branch of the stately maple tree outside her window. Sighting the first robin of the year was always a sure sign that spring was just around the corner.

It was Sunday, Mary's favorite day of the week. She was usually allowed to sleep a little later than on other days. After breakfast she and Philip walked to church. Sometimes Sarah would join them, other times not. Mary looked forward to Sunday services at the small white church located near her school. She enjoyed seeing all the people gather together. They usually took time to talk with each other, including her friends from school. She especially enjoyed the music. The hymns were so familiar to her that she could sing most of them without looking at the hymnal. Sometimes the memorable tune of a hymn would stick in her head and replay over and over throughout the day.

Mary noticed Philip in the yard and watched him as he carried a small travel bag to the outbuilding and stable that housed the horse and buggy. Mary wrinkled her nose and looked quizzically, as he disappeared through the door of the stable. He hadn't mentioned that he was going on a trip, and she wondered if that meant that they wouldn't be going to church today.

Mary changed into her favorite light-blue-print Sunday dress with a high collar and crocheted lace at the edge. A ruffle at the bottom of the skirt swung gently about her knees as she walked. Grandma had made the dress for Mary and given it to her for Christmas. It was beautiful and fit her so well. She remembered how surprised and delighted she was when she unwrapped it on Christmas Day.

Mary brushed her hair and tied it back with a large blue bow that she pulled from the top drawer of her dresser. She walked into the hallway and then down the wooden stairs to the kitchen. It was so quiet in the house. Usually on other Sundays, Sarah would be preparing breakfast, but she was nowhere around. Mary stepped up on the small wooden stool and reached the white glass water basin on the counter. She washed her face and hands and then dried them with the towel that hung from the peg on the wall nearby. She stepped down from the stool, just as Philip opened the door to the house and walked into the kitchen. He wasn't wearing the suit that he normally wore when they went to church.

"Good morning, Papa."

"Good morning, Mary."

"Papa, why aren't you dressed for church? We're going to church this morning, aren't we?"

Philip stood deathly still. He appeared frozen.

"Papa, Papa. Are you all right?"

Philip shook his head and blinked his eyes. He looked as though he was worlds away. "Mary, why don't you eat your breakfast? I have some work to do this morning. We won't be going to church today."

The look on Mary's faced showed her disappointment. "Oh, Papa. I was looking forward to church today. It's almost Easter. Are you sure we can't go?"

Philip ignored Mary's question. Instead, he went to the counter and sliced a couple pieces of bread wrapped in a white flour sack towel. Mary could smell the fresh aroma of the bread baked early in the morning. The glass jelly jar was on the table. Philip poured Mary a glass of milk and carried it to the table with the bread.

Mary ate a slice of the warm bread and berry jam. Philip stood at the counter with his back turned toward Mary. Philip was a quiet man and didn't speak often. He was particularly quiet this morning.

"Papa, can I go visit Grandma after I finish breakfast if we aren't going to church. I haven't been to visit her for several days.

Philip turned quickly, looked at Mary and spoke sharply, "No, you need to stay home. Your mother went to visit Grandma this morning, and she doesn't need you underfoot." Sarah's mother still lived in the upstairs apartment of the house across the street, although it was becoming increasingly more difficult for her to climb the steep stairs to her apartment.

Mary disliked it when her father referred to Sarah as her mother. She was anything but a mother to her. For the most part, she ignored Mary much of the day, as long as the chores were getting done. Sarah was a ruthless woman with a very cold, bitter nature. Nothing ever seemed to please her and rarely did she smile. The only time Mary ever remembered hearing her laugh was when the boyfriends visited at night, but thankfully those days were over. No men had come to visit her since that terrible night when Philip made a surprise visit home from work one evening and found a man in the house with Sarah.

Mary finished eating and started for the stairs. She should probably take off her good dress if they weren't going to church. She wouldn't want anything to happen to it.

"Where are you going?" Philip asked. Mary turned quickly. She was surprised by the sharpness in her father's voice. Philip glared at Mary and asked her again, "Where are you going?"

"I was going to my room to change my dress. I'm going to clean up the kitchen, and I don't want to get my dress dirty."

"Don't change your dress, Mary. We're going on a little trip today. You can wear that dress."

"Where are we going, Papa? Are we going to visit someone?"

Philip stood still. He looked frozen like a statue. He stuttered as he began to speak. His words came slowly and were deliberate. "Well, well, you see . . . Oh, never mind."

Mary didn't know what to do. Her father seemed upset and nervous. She had never seen him like this before. He started to pace back and forth like a cat trying to escape the room. Just then, Sarah returned. Philip and Sarah glared at one another. They were telling each other something without speaking, the way that married couples do.

"Is your mother all right?" Philip asked Sarah. "How did she handle the news?"

"Oh, Mother's all right. She'll get over it in time. She's a strong woman. Don't worry about her. Did you tell Mary, yet?"

"Tell me what?" Mary asked.

Philip and Sarah exchanged glances. "Philip, you mean you didn't talk to her? You said you'd talk to her before I came home." Sarah barked at Philip, visibly upset with him.

"I'll go upstairs and pack her things while you talk to her." Sarah stormed out of the room. Her heavy shoes made a loud noise as she stomped up the wooden stairs.

"Papa, why is she packing my things? Am I going somewhere? Where am I going, Papa?" Mary was very troubled. Obviously, her father and Sarah understood each other as they spoke.

"Mary, sit down." Philip didn't wait for Mary to move before he picked her up and set her on a wooden kitchen chair. Her short legs dangled freely. Philip bent down on his knees and sat back on his feet as he took Mary's hands in his. Her tiny white fingers looked so small in his rough calloused hands. "Mary," Philip paused and cleared his throat. "Mary, I . . . I . . . this is the hardest thing I've ever done."

"What is, Papa?" She looked at the large tears that filled his dark brown eyes.

"Your mother is upstairs packing a bag for you with your things. We're going on a trip out in the country today."

Mary was excited to hear that they were going on a trip but wondered who they were going to visit. She gazed at Philip who was visibly upset.

His voiced cracked as he started to speak. "We're taking you to the State School Orphanage today, Mary. That will be your new home."

Mary cocked her head in question. She was familiar with the orphanage that was located just outside of the town of Owatonna. She had heard people in town talk about the orphanage and the children who lived there. "Papa, I don't need to go to the orphanage? The orphanage is a place for children that don't have any family. I have you. You're my father, and I don't want to leave our house. I don't want to leave you."

"Mary, there won't be an argument. Our decision is made. Your mother is packing your things now. I have the horse and buggy ready to go, and we'll be leaving as soon as she's done packing."

"Papa, Papa, please don't take me away. I don't want to leave you. I missed you so much when you took me to live with the Clausens. I don't want to leave you again," Mary said as she started to cry. Tears streamed down her cheeks. She sniffled and wiped her nose with the back of her hand. "I promise you that I'll be very, very good, Papa, if I can stay here with you. I'm sorry if I haven't been good. I promise I'll always do my chores and I'll never ever complain. Please, please don't take me away. I don't want to leave," Mary begged.

"It'll be better for you at the orphanage. You'll have other children your age to play with. You'll be able to go to school every day."

"But I go to school every day, now, Papa, and I don't need other children to play with. I have Lizzie. She's the only one I need."

"Don't argue with me, Mary. Our decision has been made."

Mary sobbed as she sat on the chair. Tears soaked the front of her pretty blue dress. Philip pushed himself up from the floor and slowly walked across the kitchen. He paused as he opened the door to the backyard but then continued on. He left the door open behind him. Mary watched as he sank onto the wooden bench at the side of the old stable. Philip rested his elbows on his knees and placed his face in his hands. His shoulders shook as he wept.

Mary walked to the doorway. "Papa, Papa," she screamed to him from the house. "Papa, Papa, please don't take me away. I don't want to leave you."

Philip stood up from the bench. Mary hoped that he was coming back to the house to tell her that he had changed his mind. Instead, he walked into the stable with his head hung low on his chest. He ignored Mary's tearful plea.

Sarah carried a large travel bag and a suitcase. She nudged Mary aside as she opened the screen door. Mary watched the large woman as she walked the path to the stable. Philip took the luggage from her and placed it in the back of the buggy. A single tear ran down Mary's cheek. Suddenly, Mary thought about Lizzie and ran to her room. She stopped in the doorway and was shocked by what she saw. The drawers to her bureau hung open and empty. Her closet was bare, except for a couple of old blankets and a feather tick that she used when it was very, very cold in the winter. Mary glanced quickly around her room. Lizzie wasn't there. She was sure that she left Lizzie on the bed when she went down to breakfast earlier. She lifted the bed skirt and looked under the big iron bed but Lizzie wasn't under the bed either. Panicking, she tore back the quilt on the bed and pulled the bedcovers onto the floor. Again, she looked under the bed and checked all the empty drawers and behind the bureau. Lizzie was nowhere to be found. Mary ran from her room, down the stairs and into the kitchen. With a full head of steam, she ran into Sarah.

"Where's Lizzie? I can't find Lizzie? Did you take my doll? Where is she?" Mary screamed in horror. "I can't find her," she cried.

"I put her in the buggy. She's waiting for you out there. Her scarf is out there, too."

Mary gave a quick sigh of relief. She darted around Sarah's large body and ran to the buggy. Lizzie was lying on the buggy seat. The black-and-yellow scarf that Aunt Minnie had knit for her was resting on top of the doll. Mary climbed into the buggy and grabbed Lizzie and held her close to her. Carefully, she wrapped the black-and-yellow woolen scarf around the doll's body. "Oh, Lizzie I was so afraid that they were going to take me to the orphanage without you. I promise I'll take care of you, Lizzie, wherever we are. Don't ever leave me. Please don't ever leave me." Mary pulled the doll close to her and rocked it in her arms. Lizzie was her closest companion.

Philip stood quietly by the side of the buggy. Sarah pulled the heavy wooden door of the house closed behind her. The screen door slammed shut with a bang. She walked slowly down the path to the stable. "Are we ready to leave, Philip? Help me into the buggy."

Philip walked around to the far side of the buggy and extended his hand for Sarah to climb into the buggy. Sarah wore the hat that she wore when she went to church, and she wrapped a large knitted shawl over her broad shoulders. Sarah handed Mary her winter coat. "Here, put this on. It may be a chilly ride. Don't want you to get cold."

Philip climbed into the wagon and took the worn reins in his strong, weathered hands. "Mary, it's time to go. Sit down. I don't want to you to get hurt."

Without speaking a word, Mary climbed onto the seat between her father and Sarah. She didn't particularly want to sit next to either of them but moved closer to her father. Philip snapped the reins, and the horse and buggy moved slowly down the street. Mary glanced over her shoulder at their house and wondered if she would ever come back.

"Papa, I'm scared. I don't want to leave you. I don't want to live at the orphanage."

"Mary, that's enough," Philip said sharply. "I'm not going to talk about it anymore. It's what's best for you. There are many, many people who would like to have a little girl like you."

Sarah looked straight ahead with no expression on her face. She didn't speak. Philip glanced at her, but she didn't acknowledge his look.

"Mary, you were an orphan from the beginning, and you will always be an orphan."

Mary heard Sarah's words but didn't understand what she was saying. Mary knew that she had been an orphan a long time ago because her mother had abandoned her at the church home in St. Paul, but then Philip and Josie adopted her. Didn't that mean that she was no longer an orphan? Or, if people became an orphan, were they always orphans, even if someone adopted them? *Besides*, she wondered, *what's wrong with being an orphan?* As far as she could tell she was no different from any of the other children she knew who had two parents. So, what made her different?

"Will I still be an orphan if someone adopts me from the orphanage, Papa?"

Philip wasn't sure of the correct reply and ignored Mary's question. Mary repeated the question to her father. "Will I always be an orphan?" Mary looked at her father in question.

"Mary, you'll always be an orphan. Your mother didn't want you when you were a baby, so she gave you away. Once an orphan, always an orphan." Sarah's words were sharp and bitterly cold.

Philip glared at her. Sarah stared straight ahead and didn't speak another word during the rest of the trip.

ဏ 13 ௧

LARGE CLUMPS OF MUD LIFTED from under the horse's feet as it walked on the dirt road saturated with water from the rapidly melting snow. Small farms with vast, vacant fields dotted the rolling countryside. Before long spring planting would begin, and the landscape would quickly change into bright colors of green and gold. At one farm, Mary could see several children playing with a black-and-white dog in the yard. The dog barked as it nipped at the children and chased them through the yard. She could hear their playful laughter faintly in the distance and silently wished that she could join in the fun. *Oh, how much fun it would be to have a brother or sister,* Mary thought as she looked at the children with envy—*there would always be someone to play with.*

As they ascended the road, a very large reddish-brown brick building came into view on the horizon. The pointed top of a tall brick turret appeared first. It looked like a witch's hat on top of a round brick tower with several oval-shaped windows. Soon, the entire estate was visible. The largest building—the one with the turret—was surrounded by several smaller buildings that were constructed of the same type and color of brick.

"Papa, look. Look at that," Mary said as she pointed her finger at the building in the distance. It was the biggest building Mary ever remembered seeing. "Who lives in that house? It's so big," she declared. "It must be a king and a queen." Philip ignored her question as he drove the wagon straight ahead.

The building housed the Minnesota State Public School for Dependent and Neglected Children. It was created by the Minnesota legislature in 1885. Construction was completed in December 1886. Approximately five percent of the children were orphaned—they had no parent. Most of the children were simply deserted. The school served as an interim institution for children to ensure that they were in good health, educated, and given Christian training. The goal was to move the children into homes via adoption or indenture. Owatonna was chosen for the site of this state-of-the-art institution because it was near the center of the most densely populated rural area of the state. It also had easy access to railroads.

The cottage-style campus orphanage sat on one hundred and sixty acres of land on the outskirts of Owatonna, a city of fifty-five hundred people located about sixty miles southwest of St. Paul, the capital city of Minnesota. The three-story main building of the orphanage was constructed of reddish-brown brick and housed the reception room, superintendent's office, staff offices, library, chapel, children's and employees' dining rooms, industrial departments, and a small boy's living quarters. The upper floors provided living area for employees. There were three orphans at the orphanage when it was first opened. Eventually it housed as many as five hundred children in sixteen cottages of about thirty children each and one hundred staff. One matron lived full-time in each of the cottages.

The orphanage, or State School, as it became to be known, was in a world of its own. It was a self-sustaining institution with its own dairy barn, fields, pastures, animals, nursery, hospital, and even a cemetery. It had its own farm operation with cows, chickens, horses, and pigs. They grew much of their own food. One building had a huge root cellar in the basement. The basement smelled like rotting food. It kept produce available through the non-growing season. The bakery, in the basement of the building across the hall from the root cellar, subdued the rotten smell. In 1904 a fire destroyed the main building of the orphanage. It was rebuilt in 1905.

The children at the State School held jobs to help sustain the orphanage. Boys, about age twelve, worked in the cow barns, horse barns, and farm fields. Older boys worked in the bakery. A group of young girls worked in the dining room where the matrons ate, while others helped prepare food or cleaned dishes in the kitchen.

Mary looked on in awe as Philip drove the buggy closer and closer to the castle-like building. Smaller buildings, called cottages, dotted the huge estate. A group of about thirty children, all girls, marched in single file, one right after the other, from the big building to one of the small cottages. They were dressed similarly in dark, woolen coats and hats and looked straight ahead as they marched. Long skirts showed at the bottom of their coats. Their legs were covered with long black stockings. The girls didn't speak as they filed, one by one, into the cottage. They were followed by a group of about thirty boys. They, too, walked in single file, followed by a matron. A small boy, whose bright white curls stuck out around the edges of his hat, poked at the back of the boy in front of him. The matron, whose job was to demand absolute obedience from the children, saw the boy's misbehavior and promptly reprimanded him with the long narrow wooden brush that she carried in her right hand. The boy immediately put his hands at his side and looked straight ahead as the line of children marched single file into another cottage.

Philip drove the wagon to the back side of the large main building. He hooked the reins of the horse to an iron ring on top of a wooden pole, then walked to the other side of the wagon and helped Sarah to the ground. Sarah smoothed her shawl with her hands and adjusted her hat.

Mary didn't move. She sat firmly on the wooden wagon seat and gazed into the grassy courtyard that was surrounded by a grove of mature trees at the back of the building. It looked like a pleasant place for summertime picnic.

Philip extended his arms. "Mary, I'll help you down," he said to her in a quiet voice. Mary ignored Philip. She didn't move. "Mary, Mary," Philip shouted, "did you hear me? I said come over here so I can help you down."

"I told you, Philip, the child never does what she's told," Sarah glared at Mary. "Mary," Sarah said sharply, "do as your father tells you, or I'll get a switch off the tree and use it on your backside. That'll get your attention and make you move."

Mary ignored Sarah. She doubted that Sarah would live up to her threat as long as Philip was standing there, although Mary had been at the receiving end of Sarah's quick temper many times before.

Philip extended his arms to Mary again. This time she slowly slid across to the edge of the wagon seat. Lizzie, wrapped in her black-and-yellow scarf, was firmly in Mary's grip. Philip hoisted Mary to the ground while she continued to look straight ahead.

"We need to talk with the head superintendent of the school. He knows we're coming and should be expecting us."

Mary heard Philip's comment to Sarah. She wondered how long they had been planning on taking her to the orphanage. She was sure that this was something that Sarah had suggested to Philip. Sarah never wanted her around, unless there was some work to be done.

Philip and Sarah walked side by side on the stone walk that led to the large, wooden double door at the front of the building. A huge concrete arch extended over the entryway. Mary walked close to Philip's side. She paused as she bent her head back and looked up at the turret with the funny looking witch's hat on top. It was a long ways up. *Must be a special princess who gets to live in this part of the building*, she thought.

"Mary, Mary," Philip called. "Come along. Stop daydreaming." Philip held the front door open for Mary. Sarah was already inside the large entry of the building.

"May I help you," a woman said to Philip and Sarah as she approached. The woman's shoes made a loud sound that echoed as she walked with authority across the tiled floor in the foyer. She stopped in front of Philip. Her back was straight, and she clasped her hands behind her back. Her sharp-featured face was stern and unfriendly looking.

"How do you do? I'm Philip Sutton." Philip clutched his wool winter cap tightly in his hands and pressed it against his chest. "This is my wife, Sarah." He cast a polite look in Sarah's direction. Sarah nodded her head. She held her hands tight in front of her. The cold expression on her face didn't change.

"The superintendent is expecting you. I'll show you to his office. I hope you had a pleasant trip. You certainly had wonderful weather. I think we're going to have an early spring this year."

Mary followed Philip and Sarah while they walked alongside the stern-looking woman. She escorted them to a room on the right side of the beautiful foyer. It was so clean. It gleamed. The floor shone brilliantly, just like glass. The woman pushed open the large wooden door to the superintendent's office. She motioned for Philip, Sarah, and Mary to enter the room.

A bald man, dressed in a dark-gray, pinstripe suit, sat behind the desk at the far side of the stately room. He had a very round face and pale complexion. Small round spectacles rested at the end of his pudgy nose. A window behind his desk looked out into the grassy area where they had tied the horse and buggy. He stood up from the desk as they entered the room and extended his hand to Philip. "Hello, I'm Superintendent Hagen."

Nervously, Philip tucked his hat into the pocket of his coat and extended his hand. "Hello, Mr. Hagen. I'm Philip Sutton. This is my wife, Sarah."

"Please, have a seat, Mr. and Mrs. Sutton. I have a few papers for you to sign. It won't take but a few minutes, and then you can be on your way. I know you have a rather long trip to get back to the city. I don't want to keep you too long."

Philip and Sarah sat in the upholstered straight-back chairs, opposite Superintendent Hagen. Mary leaned tightly against the arm of her father's chair. She gazed quickly around the room. Superintendent Hagen looked at the papers that sat in front of him on the desk. He fumbled through them, put a couple to the side and then looked up over his tiny spectacles. "Mr. and Mrs. Sutton, you understand that by leaving your child at the Minnesota State Public School for Dependent and Neglected Children she becomes a permanent ward of the State of Minnesota. Do you understand that?"

Philip and Sarah nodded silently in agreement.

"Please tell me her name, so I can enter it on these papers for you to sign."

"Her name is Mary. Mary Sutton," Philip said softly with a crack in his voice.

Superintendent Hagen picked up a long slender pen and dipped it quickly in a small black bottle of ink. The pen made a scratching noise when he wrote on the paper. He turned the page over, pushed it aside, and dipped the pen in the ink bottle again. He wrote on two more sheets of paper. Each time he turned the paper over and placed in on top of the previous one.

"Now, I'll need you to sign at the bottom of each of these papers." He turned the papers to Philip, dipped the pen in the ink bottle and handed it to Philip. He pointed. "Please sign here and here."

Hesitantly, Philip pulled the papers closer to him. He took a deep breath and paused briefly. It was deathly quiet in the room. Bright sunshine beamed through the window and brightened the room. The slender pen looked small in Philip's large hand. The only sound was the scratching noise when Philip signed his name on the papers.

The woman who had directed them to Superintendent Hagen's office stood at the back of the room. She took a few steps forward and approached the desk. "Child, you need to come with me," she said.

Mary turned quickly when the woman spoke. She cast a horrified look at the woman. "Papa, Papa," she cried. "Papa, I don't want to leave you. Please take me home with you. I want to go home with you. I don't want to stay here. Please don't leave me here," she begged. Mary grabbed the arm of the chair where Philip sat. The knuckles on her tiny hands turned white, as she held tight. Lizzie was tucked securely under one of her arms.

"Child, come," the woman demanded. She tugged on Mary's coat sleeve and tried to pull her away from Philip. Mary cried and continued to plead with Philip. Finally, the woman pulled hard at Mary's arm. Lizzie slipped out and fell to the floor. Mary let go of the arm of the chair to retrieve her doll. Like a cat, the woman snatched Lizzie from the Mary's grasp. With tears streaming down her cheeks, Mary begged, "Please, may I have my doll? Please let me hold Lizzie."

"I'll let you hold your doll, but you need to come with me."

Mary looked at Philip and then looked back at the woman. She looked back and forth several times. She knew that she wasn't going to win this argument. Reluctantly, she followed the woman as she led her from the room. Mary looked back one last time. Philip's head hung low. His chin rested on his chest.

"Good-bye, Papa," Mary said. She put her hand in the air, gave a quick wave, and followed the woman out of the room.

❧ 14 ☙

THE SIGN ON THE OUTSIDE OF THE DARK brick cottage read: "COTTAGE NO. 12." It was called the detention cottage. All children who were new to the orphanage were required to spend two to three weeks at Cottage No. 12 when they arrived. They were given shots for contagious diseases. Their clothing was removed; they were deloused and then given different clothing. There were only a few children in Cottage No. 12 when Mary arrived. Miss Leary, a tall, slender woman with bright orange hair the color of a carrot, was the matron of Cottage No. 12. She was middle-aged and had worked at the State School for many years. She was a nurse and always wore a white dress and apron.

Mary arrived at Cottage No. 12 and was directed to a large dormitory-style room. Single beds lined the perimeter of the room. Each bed was neatly made with a gray-colored blanket and pillow.

"Mary, this is the room where you and the other children sleep. Each child has a bed. This bed is yours." Miss Leary picked up the small white canvas bag with two handles lying at the end of the bed. "This is your bag, Mary. Every child has one. When you're not using your things, you put them in the bag. We need to keep the cottage clean and your things put away at all times. Use this bag. It should always be hung on the back of your chair." Miss Leary pointed her bony index finger at the white ladder-back chair at the end of the bed. "Give me your coat and hat Mary." Mary took off her hat and coat and handed them to Miss Leary. She shoved Mary's hat into the sleeve of her coat and clutched the tiny coat in her hand. "Now, follow me."

Miss Leary's long legs moved quickly. Mary almost ran to keep up with her. There wasn't a second to spare to look at her new surroundings. She was curious but would have to look at the room another time.

They walked swiftly to the room at the end of a long hall. Miss Leary opened the door, and Mary peered inquisitively inside. It was a very small, strange looking room. There was a long, narrow metal table on tall legs in the center of the room. The table had a shelf at one end that held a metal basin. A couple of metal cans with spouts sat on the floor near to the table. They looked like the cans that Philip used to fill the lanterns with fuel. A pile of rags and a couple of folded towels were on a counter next to a water basin and a large bar of soap. A very large woman dressed in a loose-fitting gown, much like a night dress, stood at the edge of the table.

"Miss Wilson, this is Mary Sutton. She arrived at the orphanage earlier today. She needs to be deloused," Miss Leary said. Miss Wilson nodded but didn't speak. The expression on her face didn't change. "Mary we need to be sure that you didn't bring any lice with you that might infect the other children. Miss Wilson will disinfect your hair and inspect your body. Take off your shoes and all your clothes. Leave them on the floor, and I'll take them away. We'll give you new clothes to wear."

Slowly, Mary bent over and untied her shoes. She sat on the floor and pulled them off, and then removed her long stockings. She looked up at Miss Leary and Miss Wilson, who were watching her. They appeared impatient. Mary stood up and quickly unbuttoned the front of her favorite blue dress. "May I keep this dress, please," Mary asked meekly. "It's my favorite dress. My Grandma made is special for me. Please?" she begged.

Miss Leary and Miss Wilson glared at Mary. "No, you can't keep your dress," Miss Wilson said sharply. "You're at the orphanage now, and you'll be treated just like the other children. They all dress the same. No one's special here. Hurry up and get undressed now," Miss Wilson demanded.

Mary continued to unbutton her dress. Miss Wilson didn't look like the type of person she wanted to argue with. It probably wouldn't get her far anyway. Silently, Mary took off her dress and under dress and dropped them to the floor. Miss Lewis picked up her clothes, opened the door to a closet, and threw them inside. Quickly, she shut the door. Mary looked in horror as her favorite blue dress disappeared from sight. Tears filled her eyes and rolled down her cheeks. As soon as Miss Leary noticed Mary's tears, she took a wooden brush and swatted it once across Mary's bare buttocks. Mary turned quickly with surprise and glared at Miss Lewis. "We don't allow crying around here. You might as well get used to it right away. If you don't, there'll be more swats with a switch or a radiator brush." Miss Lewis shook the long slender brush with stiff wire bristles at Mary.

Mary dried the tears from her face with the back of her hand. She tried hard not to cry, but her lower lip quivered. Mary rubbed her buttocks, trying to take away the sting. She didn't want to be hit again. Miss Wilson grabbed Mary under her arms, lifted her quickly, and set her on the metal table. It was very hard and cold.

"My, you are a little bit of a thing. How old are you?"

"I'm seven," Mary said.

"Oh, you can't be seven, you're much too small."

"I was born on May 17, 1898. I'll be eight in a couple months."

Miss Lewis didn't seem to be impressed by Mary's reply. She ignored Mary's comment.

"Lie down on your back and hang your head over the end of the table. I'm going to pour kerosene in your hair. We need to kill the lice if you brought any with you." Hesitantly, Mary reclined on the table. Chills ran up her spine. Her head hung uncomfortably off the end of the table. "Close your eyes tight and hold your breath. Don't breathe and don't open your eyes until I tell you. If you get kerosene in your eyes, it will make you go blind. If you drink any, it'll kill you."

Mary squeezed her eyes closed tight and took a deep breath. Miss Wilson picked up the metal container of kerosene and placed the spout on the center of Mary's forehead. Kerosene flowed from the can, through Mary's bright curls and into the basin. Fumes filled the air of the room. Mary didn't move. She kept her eyes shut tight. Kerosene filled her ears.

"You can breathe now, but keep your eyes closed. I'm going to rinse your hair with water."

Mary choked when she took her first breath. The kerosene fumes were so thick, it was difficult to breathe. Miss Wilson poured cool water through Mary's hair and then dried it with a towel. The cool water on Mary's scalp sent shivers through her tiny body.

"Open your eyes. Sit up." Mary sat up. Drops of liquid ran down her back. "Now, I'm going to give you an injection. We can't have any sick children. One sick child is all it takes to start an epidemic here at the orphanage."

Miss Wilson lifted the lid of a small metal box on the counter. She removed a hypodermic needle and injected Mary quickly. Mary gasped. The injection surprised her more than it hurt. It happened so quickly.

Miss Leary grabbed Mary under her arms, lifted her from the table, and placed her on the floor. The tile floor was cold under Mary's bare feet. Gooseflesh covered her body. A stack of folded clothing sat on the wooden chair near the door of the room. Black stockings poked out of the top of the small brown boots on top of the pile.

"These are your clothes. Get dressed. I'll take you back to your bed. It's almost time for dinner."

Mary was freezing cold and dressed as quickly as she could. The kerosene fumes in the room were overwhelming and made it difficult to breathe. She slipped on her under dress and pulled the washed-out gray-colored dress over her head. It was at least a size too large, but she should grow into it. It felt warm to cover her body. She tugged at the long black stockings while she sat on the floor and laced up her new boots. They were well-worn but fit her well. Mary followed Miss Leary to the dormitory.

"This is your bed. This is your chair. Here is your bag. Sit on your chair and fold your hands on your lap. You'll be called for dinner in about forty-five minutes."

Obediently, Mary sat on the hard wooden chair. Her short legs dangled freely. She straightened her dress and looked down at her new boots.

"Sit still, Mary. No fidgeting. Put your hands on your lap and fold them," Miss Leary said sternly. She tapped the wooden radiator brush on Mary's shoulder, sending a silent message to Mary as she left the room. Obviously there were going to be many new rules to learn. She already found out that disobeying wasn't an option.

Mary sat quietly as she had been directed. Since there wasn't anything left to do but wait, Mary sat patiently and looked curiously about the room. There wasn't much to see, just beds and white ladder-back chairs with bags hung over the backs. After fifteen minutes, a row of ten children marched single file into the room. Their shoes landed hard on the wooden floor. Each child took a seat on a chair at the end of a bed. They folded their hands and sat quietly. The silence was deep. No one spoke. No one stirred. It was one of the rules at the orphanage. The children maintained an ominous silence for one-half hour before breakfast, lunch, and dinner. If anyone disobeyed, the matron who stood guard at the door was swift to make a correction with a radiator brush or wooden ruler. Finally, after thirty minutes, the matron returned and looked sternly into the room. The silence was broken by her call to the children, "Dinner," she called. "Line up and march single file."

The children obediently followed her instruction. They stood in a single line, one right behind the child before. Mary slipped off her chair. She wasn't sure what was happening or where exactly she was going but she followed along. Mary stood directly behind a tall, brown-haired girl in front of her. The line started to move. As they approached the doorway, the girl in front of Mary spoke. "I'm Mabel. What's your name?" the tall girl whispered out of the corner of her mouth.

"I'm Mary Sutton," she whispered. Mary kept her eye on the matron at the front of the line. She wanted to be sure that the matron didn't catch her talking.

"We're going to the dining hall for our noon dinner. Follow along. We're not allowed to speak at dinner. We'll have some time to play this afternoon. It's Sunday. We can talk then."

Mary continued to look straight ahead. The line of children marched into a large building nearby and down a long hallway. The aroma of food permeated the air. Mary put her nose in the air, took a deep breath, and let it out slowly. It had been a long time since she ate. Her stomach had been making grumbling noises for quite a while.

The children entered a large room with several wooden tables set in rows, end to end. White wooden chairs were pushed up to each table. There was a place setting of dishes and a drinking glass on the table in front of each chair. Several other children already in the room stood silently next to the white wooden chairs. They all looked straight ahead. No one spoke. The children in Mary's group marched to a table at the near end of the room and separated from the other children. Mary followed precisely behind Mabel, who stood next to a chair. Mary did the same. They stood silently for about a minute. A loud bell broke the silence. Each child pulled a chair away from the table. The noise of chairs scraping across the tiled floor echoed in the sterile-looking room. All the children sat straight on their chairs and folded their hands on the table in front of them. The loud bell rang a second time. It was a signal for prayer, and the children immediately bowed their heads in prayer. Mary followed their lead. She bowed her head as if to pray. She was most curious to know where the sound of the bell came from, though. Mary peeked up. She saw a matron standing near the door. She didn't want to get caught looking up so she immediately closed her eyes and rested her head on her folded hands. Silently she said the table prayer that they said before each meal at home.

Mary thought about Papa and Sarah. They were probably still in the wagon on their way home. Just then, the bell rang again. Mary lifted her head. Several women entered the room carrying large, steaming bowls of food. The smell of potatoes saturated the air. A woman came to their table and poured each child a full glass of milk. A large bowl of potatoes and another bowl of cooked carrots was set on the table. A plate of meat that looked like sliced pork was passed around the table. Mary took a slice of meat, placed it on her plate, and set the plate of meat on the table. There wasn't much left. Probably not enough for seconds. The potatoes and carrots were also passed around the table. When everyone at Mary's table had taken some of each food, they began to eat. No one spoke. They concentrated on their eating. After twenty minutes, the loud bell clanged.

The children stood next to their chairs. All the children pushed their chairs under the table, turned, and formed a line. As soon as the bell rang again, the children marched single file from the room. Once again, Mary didn't know where she was going. Mary and Mabel exchanged a quick look but didn't speak. As they exited the room and filed into the hallway, Mary noticed a group of girls, probably about thirteen years old standing outside the dining hall. They wore dresses like the other children. Each had a white apron tied about her waist. They carried a pail, a scrub brush, and a rag. As soon as the room was emptied, the team of young girls entered and began scrubbing the white-tiled floor. The floor of the dining hall was scrubbed after every meal.

The children marched in silence back to Cottage No. 12. There was a board with wooden pegs inside the door to the cottage. The children took a coat off the peg and put it on. Mary stood still. "Do you have a coat, Mary?" Mabel asked. "Where's your coat?"

"I don't have one," Mary said with a worried look on her face. "They took it away with my other clothes when I came here today."

"We're going outside to play for a while. We always do on Sunday afternoons if the weather's nice."

Mary wasn't sure what to do. She wasn't sure if she even wanted to go out to play with the other children anyway. She really wanted to escape the orphanage and go back home. But, if she didn't even have a coat, that most certainly wasn't going to happen. She looked longingly at her bed at the far end of the room. She could see Lizzie was tucked inside her bag that hung on the back of her chair. The doll's head and one corner of her black-and-yellow scarf poked from the top edge of the bag. Mary started to walk into the room but stopped when she heard Mabel's loud whisper. "Mary, Mary, where are you going? It's time to go outside and play."

"I want to bring Lizzie outside with me. Lizzie's my doll. She's in my bag." Mary pointed at her chair with the white bag hanging on the back as she started to cross the room.

A loud voice broke the silence. "Where do you think you're going?"

Mary turned quickly as the matron approached her shaking her radiator brush.

"Where do you think you're going?" the woman said again. "It's time to go outside. Get your coat and go along with the other children."

Mary wasn't quite sure what to say to the matron. She didn't look like the type of person that she wanted to cross.

"Answer me," the stern-looking matron shouted in a loud crisp voice.

"I, I, I," Mary stammered. "I want to bring my doll outside with me to play. May I, please?"

The tall woman planted her large feet firmly on the floor in front of Mary.

"I want to go outside and play, too, but I don't have a coat," Mary said hesitantly.

The woman gave a loud huff and walked away quickly. Her feet pounded on the wooden floor of the cottage. Mary ran and quickly grabbed Lizzie from her bag, and then scampered back in time to meet the woman who had returned with a dark plaid wool coat. It looked worn and much too large for Mary. "Here wear this one." She said as she extended her hand with the coat towards Mary. "You can wear this one today. We'll find another for you tomorrow. Hurry, hurry. Go outside with the other children."

Mary took the coat from the woman. Hesitantly, she set Lizzie on the floor, securely between her feet and slipped on the coat. She was hoping that the matron wouldn't notice Lizzie lying on the floor. Mary grabbed her doll and scurried as quickly as she could to the outside door of the cottage. The other children had already gone outside to play. She didn't want to be left behind, but mostly she wanted to get out of the reach of the nasty-looking matron, who always carried a wooden radiator brush with her.

It felt good to get outside. Mary took a deep breath of the cool March air. The ground was damp and soggy. Small piles of snow dotted the grounds of the orphanage. The sun was doing its work, and the snow was melting rapidly. Mary gazed into the distance and fixed her eyes on the road that she had traveled with Papa and Sarah a few hours before. It wouldn't be long before they would be home. She longed to be there with them. Why did they take her to the orphanage? What did she do wrong that made them take her away, so far away? She wondered if she would ever get to see her papa again. Perhaps he would come to the orphanage for a visit someday. There were so many rules at the orphanage, though. She wondered if the people who ran the orphanage would even allow him to visit her.

Mary remembered her life with Mama and Papa. They had been a real family—a very happy family. She wished she could go back in time. Mary knew that she had been an orphan before Mama and Papa; her mama had told her that before she died. She had told her the whole story—that her real mother didn't have a husband and wasn't able to care for her alone so she brought her to a church home in St. Paul. The nuns at the home took care of her until they were able to find a family for her. One day, Papa and her mama traveled to St. Paul and adopted her.

Papa was a very different man when her mother was alive. He was happy and full of life. His spirit died when her mama passed away. It was difficult for Mary to remember her mama. She closed her eyes tight and tried to picture her mama's face, but the image became more and more faint as months and years passed.

"Mary, Mary," Mabel stood at Mary's side. "Mary, what are you doing? Why are you standing here with your eyes closed? What are you doing?"

Mabel's voice rocked Mary from her daydream. She gazed at Mabel. "Oh, I was just thinking."

"What were you thinking about? I've been calling you to come over and play with us, and you didn't move. You looked frozen as stiff as a board."

"Oh, I was thinking about my papa. I miss him terribly. I want to go home and be a family." Tears welled in Mary's eyes.

"Papa? Family? What are you talking about? You're an orphan, Mary. The only family you have now are the other orphans here at the orphanage. You're an orphan. Orphans don't have real families."

"But I did have a family. I had a father and a mother," Mary argued. "We lived in a house in the city."

"Then how did you come to the orphanage? Did you run away? Did someone pick you up and bring you here? How come you came to the orphanage?"

Mary wasn't sure how to answer Mabel's question. She wasn't exactly sure why Philip and Sarah brought her to the orphanage, although she suspected it was Sarah's idea.

"Well, you see, my first mama died. Papa remarried a new lady whose name was Sarah. I guess she didn't like me too well." Mary pondered what she wanted to say next. "I guess I was a mischief." Mary thought about Sarah and the boyfriends she sneaked into the house while her papa was at work. It was an accident that her father saw her pick up the man's glove in their backyard. She didn't plan on telling him about Sarah's boyfriends. It was a terrible accident that he found out.

Mary remembered the horrific fight that her father had with the man he caught with Sarah when he came home from work unexpectedly. Mary wondered what she could have done differently. Maybe she could have done something to prevent the whole situation. If so, she'd still be living at home with Papa and Sarah. Tears streamed down her cheeks. She fought hard to keep the tears back, but she wasn't able to. She didn't want to cry in front of Mabel or the other children. Mabel noticed Mary's tears. Gently, she put her arm around Mary's shoulder and pulled her against her side. "Mary, please don't cry. They don't allow crying here at the orphanage. You have to forget about your past. You're living at the orphanage now. Regardless of what's happened in the past, you're living here now."

Mary wiped her tears away with the sleeve of her new coat that hung far beyond the ends of her hands. Lizzie was in her hand. "Why did you come to the orphanage, Mabel?"

"We had seven children in our family. My father was a drunk. He went to the saloon almost every day. He'd come home drunk and beat my mother or sometimes us kids. One day he disappeared. Don't know what ever happened to him. He deserted my mama and us kids. She couldn't take care of all of us. Some neighbors on a farm took my two older brothers. The boys'll be able to help with the farm work. A couple of the older girls stayed with my mama. They work as maids at the hotel and can help Mama out with the living. She couldn't care for us all, so she brought me, my younger sister, Harriet, and little brother, Harvey, to the orphanage. They're twins. Guess it's all she could do. Too many mouths to feed. I haven't seen Harriet and Harvey since I got here. They must be at the cottage for the little ones because they're only two years old. I sure hope they're doing all right. I really miss them. I'm sure they miss their mama, too."

Mary listened carefully to Mabel's story. "When did you come here?"

"I've been here just over a week. In a few days, they'll move me to another cottage with girls my age. Cottage No. 12 is the detention cottage. All the new kids have to stay in detention until they know that we aren't sick and we don't have lice. Mary thought back to earlier in the day when she had been deloused with kerosene. The pungent smell of kerosene lingered in her hair even though it had been washed.

"How old are you, Mabel? Maybe we'll get moved into the same cottage."

"I'm ten years old. How old are you?"

"I'm seven, but I'll turn eight in a couple months. My birthday's in May."

Mary and Mabel watched a group of girls playing a game of tag in a grassy area in the distance. Boys played on a rope swing that hung from the branch of a huge oak tree. The boys took turns swinging from the end of the rope and soaring like birds through the air.

"We aren't supposed to play with the other kids until we get out of the detention cottage. We're supposed to keep our distance."

Mary and Mabel stood at the edge of the grassy play area and longingly watched the other children, who looked like they were having fun. They hoped it wouldn't be long before they could play with the others, too.

"I miss my papa, Mabel. I want to go home, so badly." Mary looked sadly at Lizzie as she clutched her loyal companion in her arms.

THERE WERE PLENTY OF RULES TO FOLLOW at the orphanage. Everyone followed exactly the same stringent routine. Contact with the outside world was strictly controlled for the orphans. The school didn't want any homesick children.

After two weeks at Cottage No. 12, Mary moved to Cottage No. 5. It housed about thirty girls age six years to sixteen years. Mary carried her canvas bag with Lizzie and her other possessions tucked securely inside to her new cottage.

145

Every morning, precisely at 6:00 a.m., the matron woke the children. They washed their faces and hands and then were required to sit on their chair in total silence. After about thirty minutes, the matron would give them the instruction to change clothes. The children stood next to their chairs as they changed into their clothes. They folded their night clothes and placed them in the bag on the back of their chair. Quickly, they formed a single-file line and marched about a block to the dining hall for breakfast. The children waited behind their chairs at the dining tables until a bell rang, and they simultaneously pulled out their chairs, sat at the table, and waited for the next bell. They bowed their heads, silently said a meal prayer, and raised their head when the next bell rang. It was the same routine before every meal of every day. The meals were the same for each day of the week. Wednesday dinner was always hash. Thursday dinner was always liver.

When the children finished their dinner, they marched in a row to their cottages. When it was time for bed, the children kneeled by their beds and said their prayers. Then the lights were out. No talking was allowed after the lights were out. If there was any whispering or talking, the cottage matron was swift to command silence again. She walked through the dark cottage and swatted each child in her bed, regardless where the talking was coming from. Mary quickly fell into the strict daily routine of the State School Orphanage.

Cottage No. 5 was more spacious than the detention cottage. The girls were getting dressed when Mary and the matron arrived. All heads turned when they entered the room. Neatly made beds surrounded the perimeter of the room with one ladder-back chair at the end of each bed. It looked just like Cottage No. 12 only there were many more beds.

Mary looked around the room. Her eyes stopped when she caught sight of Mabel, the only familiar face Mary saw. She was delighted that Mabel had been moved to Cottage No. 5, too. Mabel had moved there about one week prior.

The matron showed Mary to her bed and chair. Mary wanted to greet Mabel, but she knew talking wasn't allowed and was confident that there would be a swift and painful correction if she did. Mary and Mabel exchanged friendly smiles as she passed by.

"Today is Saturday," the matron said as Mary placed the handles of her canvas bag on the back of her chair. "Everyone needs to do chores. You'll be going to the main building after breakfast to help with the cleaning. There's a room where visitors come on Sundays. The room needs to be cleaned before tomorrow. Come to the main building directly after breakfast." The girls lined up at the cottage door. Mary slid in line right behind Mabel. They marched single file to the dining hall.

"I'm going to the main building to clean, too." Mabel turned and spoke in a soft voice, so she wouldn't get caught. "I'll show you the way." Mary smiled at Mabel and breathed a sigh of relief. It seemed that the only way to learn what you were supposed to do was to do something wrong. Correction was usually swift and strong.

After breakfast, Mary followed Mabel and two other girls from Cottage No. 5 to the main building. It was a beautiful spring day. The grass on the school grounds was breaking through the soggy earth. Swollen buds on the yellow-green leafless trees were about to pop. A red-breasted robin hopped in the yard. The bird stopped, cocked its head, paused and listened carefully. Quickly, it pecked at the earth and pulled out an earthworm. The worm wiggled as it dangled from the bird's beak.

"Look, Mabel." Mary pointed at the bird as they passed. "It's the first robin of the season. You know what that means don't you?" Mary didn't wait for Mabel to reply. "Spring is here." Mary said as she lifted her arms playfully into the air and spun herself around. "It's my favorite time of the year."

"What's so special about springtime? It's not special to me," Mabel grumbled.

"Oh, I love spring. Everything's new. Smell the air. Doesn't it smell wonderful? It's so fresh." Mary closed her eyes, breathed deep, and filled her lungs with the spring air. She slowly let the air out of her

147

lungs. When Mary opened her eyes, she noticed that the other girls were far ahead of her. She ran to catch up.

The girls walked on the paved sidewalk to the back of the large brick building. It was the building where Philip and Sarah brought Mary when they arrived at the State School. Mary paused. She thought about her papa and Sarah and wondered what they were doing. She thought about Grandma, too, and wondered if she was lonely. Sarah didn't go to see her mother very often. Mary stopped at Grandma's house more often. She always enjoyed the old lady's company, not to mention the special treats that she was served regularly. Mary gazed at the grassy yard behind the building.

"Mary, are you coming or are you going to stand there all day," Mabel called to Mary as she held open the back door to the building. "Hurry on. We have plenty of cleaning to do. Hurry on."

The girls went to a large walk-in closet at the end of a long dark hallway. They retrieved their cleaning supplies; buckets, rags, and cans of floor paste. They filled the buckets with water and walked to a room at the front of the building. Mary recognized the room on the left as the one where they met with Superintendent Hagen. The door to the room was cracked open. Mary peeked inside as they passed. She could see the top of Superintendent Hagen's round, bald head. His spectacles rested on the end of his nose. He was thumbing through a tall stack of papers on his stately wooden desk.

The room across the hall from Superintendent Hagen's office was where visitors were entertained. The children weren't allowed into that room unless a visitor came to see one of them. The floors in the big room were polished like window glass. Heavy, dark-burgundy-colored drapes hung from wooden rods, covered the large windows that faced the front yard of the orphanage grounds. There was an upholstered couch and two straight-backed, upholstered chairs on a patterned rug in the middle of the room. A low wooden table was placed between them. It was a formal room, very different from the other spartan-looking rooms at the orphanage.

Mary carried a big stack of rags that one of the girls in the group had handed her. She followed the instructions given. She sat on the floor outside of the room with the other girls and removed her worn leather boots. Only guests were allowed to wear shoes in the visitors' room.

One of the girls began to wipe the wooden floor with a rag and water from the bucket. Another girl followed behind her and dried the floor with a rag. After a small part of the floor was cleaned, Mabel opened a metal can of floor wax and rubbed a small amount of wax on the floor. The overpowering smell of the wax saturated the room. Mary worked behind Mabel as she removed the white-colored dried wax with a rag. She polished the dark wood to a dazzling shine. The floor shone like glass, so much so, that she could see the reflection of her face in the floor.

"Have you ever been in such a beautiful room before Mabel?" Mary asked.

"The only time I've seen a room like this was when I cleaned it last week. I doubt that I'll see it any other time. Don't think anyone ever plans to visit me."

Mary continued to remove the wax from the floor. She and Mabel talked while they worked and shared experiences from their first couple of weeks at the State School. They agreed that life at the orphanage was tolerable as long as they stuck with the routine and obeyed all the rules. Learning the rules was another story. No one actually told them the rules. They were simply punished for not knowing.

A matron came to inspect their work. She examined the awesomely clean room carefully. She examined every corner. She ran her hand over the coffee table and looked for any dust that they may have missed. The girls stood still, silently hoping that their cleaning would pass her thorough inspection.

"You're free to go. Put your supplies away," the matron said as she turned on her heel and walked out of the room. The girls breathed a collective sigh of relief.

"It's almost time for our noon meal," Mabel said. "Let's put these supplies away and go back to the cottage. We can go outside and play with the other children after we eat."

The girls sat on the floor, quickly laced up their boots, and headed back to their cottage.

৯ 15 ৎ

SUMMER AT THE STATE SCHOOL ORPHANAGE was a very pleasant time of year. The weather allowed for much more outdoor activity. However, it also meant much more work. Large vegetable gardens needed to be planted and tended all over the State School grounds. Children were assigned to gardens and pulled fast-growing weeds nearly every day. Mary, Mabel, and several other girls from Cottage No. 5 worked in the garden.

"Mary, it's almost the Fourth of July. Do you know what that means?" Mary looked at Mabel curiously. She didn't understand Mabel's question. "The Fourth of July is a big holiday. We get to celebrate the birthday of the United States. All the children are invited to a big party. There's going to be a picnic outside, and we get to play games and have races with the other children. I heard that we get to have ice cream, too."

"Really? Do you think it's true?"

"I talked to Carolyn in our cottage. She was here last year. She said it was the best day of the whole year. A band played music all day long. There was a parade with red, white, and blue flags. Everyone got to ride on a hay wagon. At the end of the day, someone came and shot firecrackers, too. I can hardly wait. The Fourth of July is Wednesday, next week, which means we don't have to go to school that day. We get a whole day off, right in the middle of the week."

Mary could hardly believe what she was hearing. There usually wasn't much cause for celebration at the orphanage. As a matter of fact, her birthday passed on May 17 without notice. It was just another day of the week.

"Oh, I can hardly wait, too. I wonder if I can be in the parade. I'd like to carry the big American flag at the front of the parade."

"Don't be silly, Mary. You're too small. That flag at the front of the parade would be much too big for you to carry. If a wind came up, it would carry you into the next county."

Mary knew that she was small for eight years old. She didn't appreciate Mabel making fun of her size.

That evening after dinner, Mary went back to the cottage with the other children. They played in the cottage for a while before it was time to get ready for bed. Mary wasn't feeling very well. She was tired and ached all over. She didn't even feel like playing, so she changed into her night dress and crawled into bed. It was warm outside and even warmer inside the cottage. How come she was so cold? She couldn't seem to warm up. She curled up, rested her head on her pillow and fell fast asleep.

"Mary, Mary," the matron said. She touched Mary's shoulder. "Mary, wake up. It's time to get up. Time for breakfast." Mary rolled onto her back and opened her eyes. The matron looked at her and touched her face. "Child, you're burning up. Your bed clothes are soaked. You have a terrible fever." The matron took the blanket from Mary's bed and wrapped her securely. "You need to see the doctor." The matron lifted Mary from the bed and carried her out of the cottage. Mary didn't have the strength to lift her head. She rested her head on the matron's shoulder. The woman carried Mary to the hospital at the State School, which was a couple blocks away. A nurse dressed in a white uniform and small white cap greeted them at the door.

"Oh, who do you have here?" the nurse said as she touched Mary's forehead. "This child is burning up. She has a very high fever. Bring her this way," she said, pointing to the room next door. "Lay her on the bed. I'll get the doctor."

The matron followed the nurse into the examining room and laid Mary on the bed. The nurse left the room and returned promptly with a young man dressed in a long white coat. He had a stethoscope hung around his neck. He touched Mary's forehead and cheeks. "She has a very high fever. We need to get the fever down right away. Nurse, get some ice. We'll pack her in ice for a while. Hopefully, it will bring her temperature down quickly."

The matron and the doctor removed the blanket from Mary and took off her night dress. They wrapped her in a clean white sheet. The nurse left the room and returned with a pail filled with chopped ice. Quickly she laid ice on Mary and packed it around her sides. She soaked a small cloth in cold water, folded it, and laid it on Mary's forehead. Mary didn't move. She was far too weak. The cool rag on her forehead felt good.

"What do you think's wrong with her, doctor? Do you know what she has?"

"It's hard to say. First, we need to get her temperature down and stabilized." The doctor took Mary's temperature while the nurse tended to the ice that surrounded her. "Mary is your throat sore?" the doctor asked as he stroked her bright red cheek. "Open your mouth. I want to look inside."

Slowly, Mary opened her mouth. She coughed violently and spit up gray phlegm. The doctor looked at Mary's red throat and felt her swollen glands at the sides of her neck. "Her throat is almost swollen shut. I need to give her some medicine, but I think she'd choke on it if she tries to swallow. I'll give her an injection that should reduce the inflammation. We need to open her air passage so she doesn't suffocate.

The doctor and nurse hovered over Mary. The matron stood at the end of the bed. "We've had a couple other cases of diphtheria, doctor. Do you think this child might have diphtheria, too?" the nurse said in a quiet voice.

"You may be right. Diphtheria is an aggressive bacterium. It takes over the body very quickly. The injection should begin to work now. Try to get her fever to break. I'll come back in a while and see how she's doing."

Mary lay motionless on the hospital bed. Her head felt like it was going to burst. It hurt her throat just to breathe. After a couple hours, Mary's fever broke. The nurse changed her clothes and carried her to a room with two freshly made beds. She laid Mary on the bed and then tucked her in securely.

"Mary, try to get some sleep. Your fever broke so I think the worst is over. You need to get some rest so the fever doesn't come back."

Mary slept for several hours. When she woke, there was a girl about her age sleeping in the next bed. Mary realized that she must have been sleeping very soundly because she didn't wake when they brought the girl into her room. A nurse walked into the room. Her shoes squeaked on the white tile floor.

"Oh, looks who's awake." The nurse came over to Mary's bed and laid her hand on Mary's forehead. She touched Mary's rosy red cheek. "Your temperature has dropped quite a bit. You gave us quite the scare today, little girl."

Mary tried to speak. She wheezed, but no sound came out. Her throat was really sore.

"Would you open your mouth for me, please? I want to look inside." Obediently, Mary opened her mouth. The nurse turned Mary's head into the light and looked inside. "It's still very red in there, but at least it's not as swollen as it was when you arrived. I'm going to get you some salt water. If you gargle with salt water, it should take some of the pain in your throat away."

The nurse returned with a large glass of water and an empty white, metal pan. "Put some of the water in your mouth and swish it around. Hold your head back and make gurgling noises." Mary did as the nurse instructed, and then spit the water in the metal pan. The water was warm and tasted really salty. It wasn't very refreshing. "Keep gargling. I want you to use up all the water in the glass. The doctor asked me to find him when you were awake. I'll go find him."

The nurse returned with a man dressed in a white coat. He had dark-brown, curly hair and wore small round spectacles. He sat down on the edge of Mary's bed and took her temperature. The nurse looked on. "Looks like things are getting closer to normal," the doctor said. Your temperature was dangerously high when you came to the hospital this morning. We've had some cases of diphtheria, and I'm afraid that you have it too. You'll need to rest in bed for several days. Tomorrow morning, I'll give you another injection. We need to kill the germs in your body. If we don't, you're going to get worse again."

The doctor helped Mary lie back down in the bed. Then he left the room. The nurse tucked Mary in bed. "You do what the doctor tells you, and you'll get better. Go to sleep now. Get some rest." The nurse left the room.

Mary was exhausted. She closed her eyes and slept soundly until morning. When she woke, the doctor was examining the girl resting in the bed next to Mary. She had diphtheria, too. The doctor gave each of them an injection. The nurse handed them each a glass of salty water, asked them to gargle until it was gone, and then left the room.

Mary looked at the little girl in the bed next to her. "What's your name?" the little girl asked.

"Mary Sutton."

"I'm Carolyn Hurley."

"Is your throat sore, too?" Mary asked.

"Yes, it's very sore, and I have a headache, too."

The hospital room was on the second story of a big, brown-brick building. In the room they were in, a small window faced in the direction of the cottages on the State School grounds. Mary could see children walking in a straight line from the cottages. It must be lunch time.

"I don't like being sick," Mary said. "I'd much rather be outside. I don't want to miss school, either. I love to go to school. Reading is my favorite subject."

The nurse returned to their room. "The two of you need to get your rest. You heard what the doctor said. Lie down. I'll be back in a while to check on you."

Mary and Carolyn obediently crawled under their bed covers. The nurse tucked them in. Mary rolled over, faced Carolyn, and softly whispered, "Did you know that there's going to be a big celebration for the Fourth of July in a of couple days, Carolyn? I heard that there's going to be a big party with a parade, fireworks, and ice cream."

Carolyn didn't hear what Mary said. She had fallen fast asleep. Mary lay quietly and thought about the big celebration that the school had planned. She would never be out of the hospital by Wednesday and was very disappointed that she was going to miss the celebration. She gazed out the window at the bright sun-soaked July day. What a terrible shame to have to spend it in bed in the hospital.

In a couple of days, Mary and Carolyn were feeling much better. The nurse brought pages of newspaper and showed them how to tear the paper to make paper dolls. Mary and Carolyn decorated their room with several strings of paper dolls. After they tired of making dolls, Mary crawled into Carolyn's bed. They huddled close and giggled in the tent they had made with their with the bed covers.

"Hmmm?" Mary and Carolyn heard a woman's voice as she came into their hospital room. "Doesn't look like anyone's home in this room? Too bad, I have two big dishes of ice cream for the girls who used to be in this room. Guess I'll have to eat them myself."

Mary and Carolyn looked at each other. In unison they gasped loudly, "Ice cream!" They pulled the covers off their heads and looked at the nurse holding two dishes heaped with vanilla ice cream.

"Oh, I guess you two *are* still here. Would you like a dish of ice cream?" Mary and Carolyn looked longingly at the ice cream. "Nice to see that you're feeling better. Mary, please get in your own bed. You can each have a dish."

Although they weren't able to participate in the big Fourth of July celebration, they were delighted that they at least got to eat a dish of ice cream like the other children. The cold ice cream tasted rich and sweet and was a very special treat.

‰ 16 Œ

RED, GOLD, AND PURPLE-COLORED LEAVES blanketed the ground. Fall meant that the winter season was approaching, which also meant less time outside and more time indoors. Mary loved the out of doors. She enjoyed working in the State School gardens. Most of the children found the work tedious and boring, but it didn't bother Mary. She liked tending the garden and watching the plants grow, especially the flowers, although there weren't many. The gardens were filled mostly with vegetables to be stored in the root cellar for use during the long winter months.

The matron entered the cottage right on schedule at 6:00 a.m. She woke the children and gave them the usual instruction to wash their faces and hands. The children sat on their chairs and waited for the command to change from their night clothes and into their school clothes. Mary waited patiently on her chair with her hands folded neatly on her lap.

The matron left the room and returned with a stack of neatly folded clothing. She approached two girls seated on chairs next to each other and gave them each a new dress, shoes, and overcoat. The matron spoke to the girls, but Mary couldn't hear what she was saying. The matron crossed the room, stood in front of Mary, and extended her arms that held a blue dress, shoes, and a gray-tweed overcoat.

"Mary Sutton?"

"Yes?" Mary answered hesitantly.

"Here are some new clothes for you," the matron said as she laid the clothes and shoes on Mary's lap. "I want you to put them on." Mary looked quizzically at the matron. "You and some other children from the orphanage are going on a train today. The train will take you and the others to a new home."

Mary's was awe-stricken. She could feel her heart starting to race. "A new home?" Mary said in disbelief. "You mean I'm not going to live at the orphanage any longer?"

"That's right. You and some other children from the orphanage are going on an orphan train today. We're going to find homes for you. Change into your new clothes. After breakfast, Miss Lewis will take you and the others to the depot. Hurry on, now. Get changed."

Slowly, Mary slid off the chair. She looked across the room at the two other girls who had received new clothes. They had already changed and were sitting on their chairs. How very much Mary would have liked to ask the matron some more questions about her new home, but the matron had left the room. Mary changed clothes as she was instructed. Tentatively, she sat on her chair and waited for her next instruction. Within a few minutes, the matron came back to the room and directed the children to go for breakfast. Normally, after breakfast, Mary and the others would head off to school. Instead, Miss Lewis, another matron at the orphanage, came to the cottage. She was dressed in a long, woolen coat, knitted scarf, and carried a hat in her hand.

"Mary, Ella, and Irene. Please put on your coats and come with me. It's time for us to leave for the train."

Sadly, Mary looked around at her surroundings at Cottage No. 5. She'd been at the State School for less than nine months, but she was settled. Although life at the orphanage was very routine, Mary had adjusted well. She had made several friends and especially liked going to school every day. She was sad that she wouldn't get the chance to say good-bye to her friends or teachers.

Mary buttoned her coat over her new blue dress. She looked down at her new shoes. They were a bit big but she would grow into them. Slowly, she reached into the white canvas bag that hung on the back of her chair and pulled out her doll, Lizzie, and the black-and-yellow scarf that Aunt Minnie had knitted. Mary laid the doll in her arm, wrapped the scarf around its neck, bent over, and put her face next to the doll's body. "Oh, Lizzie, I'm scared," Mary whispered softly in the doll's ear. "I'm so scared. I don't want to leave my friends and the orphanage."

Mary walked slowly toward the doorway to the cottage. Ella, Irene, and Miss Lewis were waiting. When Mary reached the doorway to the cottage, she looked back at the room in Cottage No. 5 that had been her home. Just then, she caught sight of her friend, Mabel, who was standing next to her chair. Mabel looked so sad. Mary wanted to talk to her. She wanted to say good-bye, but there wasn't time. Miss Lewis was already far ahead with Ella and Irene.

"Good-bye, Mabel," Mary called across the room. "I hope I can see you again some day. I'll miss you." Through the tears that were swelling in her eyes, Mary could see Mabel raise her hand and give a quick wave good-bye. She ran to catch up with Miss Lewis and the others.

It was November 20, 1906, bitterly cold and very windy. Miss Lewis helped Ella, Irene, and Mary board the wagon. A boy named George was already on board. A matron from the baby cottage held an infant wrapped tightly in a thick wool blanket. The matron handed the bundle to Miss Lewis very carefully as if she was passing a basket of fresh eggs. Miss Lewis lifted the blanket, peeked inside and then put the blanket securely in place.

"Children, the driver's going to take us to the train depot. We'll board the train in Owatonna. Then we'll ride the train north for a few hours. We'll stop at some train depots along the way. We should find some families interested in taking orphaned children. We hope to find new homes for all of you."

The wind blew fresh snow in swirls on the ground. Mary and the others sat close to each other on the hard wagon seat.

"Here," the driver said, "take this blanket and put it over all of you. It should help break the wind." Miss Lewis took the blanket from the driver and passed it to Irene. Irene unfolded the blanket, laid it on the children and then slid underneath. When the driver was sure that everyone was ready, he snapped the reins, which cracked sharply in the crisp air. The wagon jolted as the horses started to walk.

Mary looked backwards several times. The State School Orphanage got smaller and smaller until it finally disappeared from view. She remembered the day Philip and Sarah had brought her there. She hadn't seen them since they left her at the orphanage several months before.

Thankfully it wasn't a very long ride to the train depot in Owatonna. The wind was cold and bit into any flesh exposed on their faces. In the distance, Mary could see the town of Owatonna. The depot, located on the opposite end of town from the house where she lived with her papa and Sarah, was coming into view. It wasn't likely that she would see either of them.

The driver stopped the wagon in front of the depot. He tied the horse's reins around a metal post. Miss Lewis handed the baby to the driver, and he held the bundle as he extended his hand to help Miss Lewis from the wagon. The baby never made a noise the entire ride.

"All right children. Get off the wagon and follow me into the depot," Miss Lewis said. "After I purchase the tickets, please walk with me to the train."

The children wandered behind Miss Lewis like a row of chicks behind their mother. They huddled together and waited for Miss Lewis inside the warm depot. When she returned, they walked side by side to the train. "Please stay together. I don't want any of you to get lost."

161

Ella and Irene, thirteen years old, had lived together in Cottage No. 5 for several years. They knew each other well and were good friends.

"Have you ever been on a train before?" Mary asked George. George's eyes were opened wide. He was trying to take in all the sites and sounds of the depot.

"No, have you?" George asked.

"I went to St. Paul once to visit my aunt," Mary said. "I was pretty small, so I don't remember much about the ride."

"I wonder where the train will take us. I hope I get to live on a farm. Maybe that way I'll get to have a dog. I had a dog before when I lived with another family. We used to play together all the time."

"I hope I get to live with a family with other children," Mary said longingly. "I want to have a big sister. I'd also like to have a brother. Maybe we'll get to live with the same family, George. Do you think that might happen?"

George looked curiously at Mary. He shrugged his shoulders. "I don't care. Just so I get to have a dog."

The children followed Miss Lewis. Outside the air was cold, the sky clear, and the bright sunshine on the snow virtually blinded them. The train conductor, dressed in a dark-blue uniform with bright gold buttons, stood at the door to the train car. He wore a small blue cap with a black visor. He extended his hand to help Miss Lewis up the three metal grate stairs on the outside of the train. Ella, Irene, and George climbed on board.

"My, you're a little thing. Here, let me help you." In one swift motion, the conductor grabbed Mary under her arms and lifted her onto the train. Miss Lewis motioned for the children to take a seat as they followed her down the aisle. After she removed her coat and hat, Miss Lewis rested the baby on her lap and pulled the blankets off its face. The baby was still sound asleep.

Mary and George sat next to each other on the hard wooden seat. George sat next to the window. Mary was seated adjacent to the aisle. She wanted to see outside so she leaned over George and peered out the window. The sky had clouded up again and snow was falling now, and the snowflakes were much larger than when they had left the orphanage. A white blanket of snow covered the ground. All of a sudden, the train whistle blew loudly three times. Mary looked out the window. She could see the train's engine at the front of the long train with white smoke billowing from the its stack. The conductor walked alongside the train. "All aboard! All aboard!" A young man and woman ran hand and hand. Out of breath, they boarded the train. They gave a deep sigh when they got on board. "All aboard!" the conductor yelled. He hopped onto the steps of the train, cupped his hand to his mouth and yelled again, "All aboard!"

The train jolted forward as it started to move slowly from the station. Mary and George looked wide-eyed at each other. The wheels made a loud clickety-clack sound at first. The train picked up speed as it traveled away from the depot and into the snowy countryside. Mary gazed out the train window and looked back at the town of Owatonna. She wondered if she would ever see her papa again or if she would ever return to Owatonna. The town became smaller and smaller until it finally disappeared from sight. She was embarking on a new adventure. Who knew what the future might bring.

The conductor walked down the aisle of the train. He patted Mary on top her head as he passed. Miss Lewis, seated behind Mary and George, handed the conductor several tickets, which he punched and then handed them back to her.

"What a good baby you have, ma'am. I haven't heard her make a peep."

"Yes, this is a very good baby. So much so that I think I might have to name her 'Baby Good,' what do you think?" The conductor chuckled at Miss Lewis' name suggestion and went on his way.

Miss Lewis stood up. She passed Baby Good to Ella and reached into a cloth bag on the seat next to her. She gave each of the children a bright red apple. Mary rubbed the apple on her coat. It shone brightly.

"Isn't it pretty, George? Have you ever seen a prettier apple?" George frowned at Mary. He'd already bit into his apple. He wiped the juice that ran down his chin on his coat sleeve.

"I'm hungry," George said. "I'm not going to look at my apple. I'm going to eat it," he proclaimed, as he took another bite. The crisp apple made a loud crack.

Mary sat back in her seat. She looked out the window as she ate her apple, too. It was sweet and very juicy. The State School Orphanage had a large grove of apple trees. Each year the apples were picked and stored in a cool cellar, so they would stay fresh long after the growing season.

After about an hour, the train left the countryside behind. Houses and buildings whisked past the window. "Look, George. We're coming to a town. Look at all the buildings," Mary said. George had his face pressed against the glass. "I've never seen such a large town before, have you?"

"No I haven't. I wonder if this is the town where we're going to get off the train."

Miss Lewis addressed the children. "Children we're coming to the depot for Minneapolis and St. Paul. The train's going to stop at the depot for a while. I want you to stay in your seats. After a short stop, the train will continue north. We have at least a couple more hours to ride."

The train blew its whistle several times as it pulled into the station. The wheels squealed loudly as the train slowed. The screech made Mary's ears hurt. She cupped her hands over her ears to protect them from the noise. The depot was constructed of dark-brown brick. The sign overhead was printed in tall black letters. It said: MINNEAPOLIS AND ST. PAUL.

"Minneapolis/St. Paul. Minneapolis/St. Paul," the conductor called as he walked down the aisle of the train and announced their arrival at the station. "Please stay seated until the train stops at the station. It'll be just a couple minutes."

The train continued to slow as it pulled into the station. Mary and George pressed their faces against the frosty window of the train car. This depot was much larger than the one in Owatonna. The train pulled under the roof of the depot building. The wheels screeched, and the train came to a jolting halt. Mary, who was still leaning over George and looking out the window, bumped him hard. George gave her an annoyed look and then looked out the window again. "Look at all the people, Mary. Have you ever seen so many people in one place before?" George asked.

"Land sakes, George. I wonder where they're all going."

Passengers began to move about in the train car. They collected their belongings and walked to the door. The conductor opened the door, lowered the metal grate stairs, and guided the passengers safely to the platform. New passengers waited patiently to board the train.

"Please stay in your seats," Miss Lewis reminded the children. "We'll be on our way again in about twenty minutes." Miss Lewis held Baby Good in her arms. The baby was living up to its name. She was awake but still hadn't made a sound. Miss Lewis instructed Irene to give each child a sandwich of bread and meat from the wicker basket under her seat. George grabbed his sandwich when Irene handed it to him and took a big bite. "Oh, this tastes good," George said as he savored the sandwich. "I was getting hungry."

Mary took a big bite of her sandwich too. Suddenly, she paused. She had been so preoccupied with the train ride that she hadn't even thought about her final destination.

"George," Mary said with her mouth full of bread, "I've been so busy looking at everything going by outside the window that I haven't even thought about where we're going. I'm scared." Mary dropped her hands onto her lap, sat motionless, and looked straight ahead. "What if there isn't a family that wants to take us? What do you think they'll do? Do you think we'll have to go back to the orphanage? I don't want to go back. I want to have a nice family with other children to play with."

"We'll just have to wait and see what happens," George said. "I know other children from the orphanage who have been taken on the orphan trains before. I don't ever remember any of them coming back."

"All aboard! All aboard!" The conductor yelled outside. His breath looked like white clouds against the cold air. He pulled up the metal stairs. The heavy metal car doors shut with a loud bang. The train jolted forward. The whistle sounded loudly three times as the train pulled away from the depot.

After an hour or so, the train stopped at the train depot in St. Cloud. Miss Lewis addressed the children again, "Children, please put on your coats and button them up. Be sure to wear your hats. Gather your other belongings and follow me."

"Do you suppose this is where a family will take us, George?" Mary said as she slipped on her wool coat. "I sure hope so." Quickly, she stuffed Lizzie into her travel bag. She walked behind George, who followed Miss Lewis up the aisle of the train. The conductor helped them off. Miss Lewis directed the children to a platform. She gathered them up, like a mother hen gathers her chicks.

"Children, some families that would like to have a child like you came to the train depot today. Please stand side by side in a row on the platform. The families will look you over. They might ask you some questions. Please answer them politely."

Mary took her place on the platform. George was on her right side and Irene on the left. Miss Lewis took her place at the end of the row of children with the baby. Several people gathered in front of the platform. "Thank you for coming today," Miss Lewis announced to the gathering crowd. "These are children from the State School Orphanage in Owatonna. They're looking for new homes. I hope you can find it in your hearts to take one or more of these children into your home. You're welcome to come closer. Talk to the children. Ask them questions if you like."

An old woman with a wooden cane moved slowly toward the platform. Her gray hair stuck out around the edges of her knit cap. She came close and put her face into Mary's. "What's your name, child?" Mary was terrified. She looked like a witch that Mary had seen in a picture book at school. The old woman, who was missing several teeth, twisted up her face into a wicked-looking mask before speaking. "Child, can you speak? I asked you your name. What's your name?" The woman's voice was raspy and cracked as she spoke.

Mary quivered. "My name is Mary."

"Speak up, child. I can't hear you. What did you say?"

"My name's Mary Sutton."

"How old are you?"

"I'm eight years old."

"Oh, you're not telling the truth. You can't be more than five or six years old. You're just a little bit of a thing."

The old lady turned and walked away. Mary breathed a heavy sigh of relief. George stood silently and looked at Mary. His eyes were open wide like saucers. "Oh, Mary, that lady scared me."

"She scared me, too," Mary said. "I'm glad that she went on her way. I'd be scared to death to live in the same house with her. She looked like a witch."

After about half an hour, Miss Lewis guided the children off the platform. She gathered them in a group around her. "Children, it's time to get back on the train. We'll stop at another station in a few minutes. Don't be discouraged, there are more families in other cities looking for children."

The children followed Miss Lewis onto the train. They took their seats, and the train pulled out of the station. A short while later the conductor stood in the aisle and shouted, "Sauk Centre! Sauk Centre!" The children followed Miss Lewis off the train. They stood in a straight row on the train platform. A young man and woman talked with Miss Lewis. They pulled away the blankets that covered Baby Good. Mary watched as Miss Lewis gave Baby Good to the young woman. She handed some papers to the young man who signed them and gave them back to Miss Lewis. The young woman never stopped looking at Baby Good. She rocked the baby back and forth in her arms and smiled. The man put his arm around the young woman's waist as they walked away.

The children followed Miss Lewis onto the train again. The next stop was Long Prairie. Irene and Ella were selected by families.

"George, Mary. It's time to get back on the train." Obediently, Mary and George followed Miss Lewis' direction. "Don't worry, you two. We have a few more stops to make. I'm sure there are wonderful families looking for children like you."

Mary and George obediently boarded the train. They took seats next to each other. Miss Lewis sat next to the aisle. Mary was fighting hard to hold back tears. She hoped that Miss Lewis and George didn't notice that she was about to start crying. She pulled Lizzie out of her travel bag and wrapped the tattered black-and-yellow knit scarf around Lizzie's neck. Mary pulled Lizzie close to her face. "Don't worry, Lizzie. Someone will take us," Mary whispered. She didn't want anyone to hear.

"Bertha! Bertha!" the conductor shouted, as he walked down the aisle.

Miss Lewis guided Mary and George off the train. They stood on the platform side by side. They waited. It was cold, and the wind blew hard. There was much more snow on the ground than in Owatonna. Mary shivered. The bitter wind bit at the tops of her bare ears. Her legs and toes were freezing cold.

Two women and a man approached the train platform. The man and woman came close to George. "What's your name?" the man asked as he looked down at George.

"I'm George Googan, sir."

"Have you ever lived on a farm or are you a city boy?"

"I'm not sure. All I ever remember is living at the orphanage. I don't remember living anywhere else."

The man reached forward and wrapped his large gloved hand around George's upper arm. "Hmmm," the man said. "You have some muscle."

"Yes, sir. I worked in the barns at the orphanage. I cleaned the barns and fed the animals every day."

"How old are you, boy?" The man's voice was very low and coarse. He bent over and looked George straight in the eye. George couldn't help but notice the man's large ears almost hidden by the flaps of his red-and-black plaid wool cap.

"I'm nine years old," George said with a crack in his voice. His knees were starting to shake. He hoped no one could see.

"You wouldn't cause me any trouble, now would ya? I've heard that some of the orphans have caused trouble. Don't want any trouble on my place."

"No, sir. I'm not lookin' to cause any trouble. Just want a home with a family. I'm a hard worker."

The man's wife stood silently behind him. She spoke to her husband as she moved forward. "Albert, I think he looks like a fine boy." She moved close to George and asked, "Is this your sister, George?" The woman pointed at Mary.

"No, ma'am. She's not my sister. Her name's Mary Sutton. She's another orphan. She's lookin' for a home, too."

Mary stood as still as she could. The wind cut through her coat. Her long black stockings offered some protection but were no match for the knife-blade wind and the icy bite of the air. She looked at the oversized lady who was examining her up and down.

"Grace, come here, look at this child." Grace Lind was Myrtle Lind's sister-in-law. Their husbands, Albert and Peter, were brothers. Grace and Peter had been married on New Years Eve, less than a year before, and they owned a farm adjacent to Albert and Myrtle. Grace was a big, hearty woman, much larger than her sister-in-law. She wore a long, dark-brown wool coat and moved side to side as she walked. The coat almost touched the tops of her old worn leather work boots, which were tied at the bottom and open at the top. Ear coverings on the side of her plaid, woolen hat flopped in the brisk wind. Small glasses with dark, round frames pressed into the skin at her temples, her eyes, behind the thick glasses made her dull greenish-gray eyes appear larger than they actually were.

Grace walked to where Myrtle and Albert stood with George at their side. Grace's large body blocked the wind from hitting Mary. It felt good to be out of the bitter wind, even for a moment. Mary lifted her head slowly and looked up at Grace. She offered a nervous little smile to the oversized woman.

"What do I want with an orphan?" Grace said sharply to her sister-in-law. "I know you and Albert need extra help on the farm and can use the boy," she said as she pointed to George, who stood nervously at Albert's side. "We could probably use an extra hand on the farm, but what would I do with a girl? She's so small that she could hardly carry a full bucket of water."

Mary didn't care for Grace's comment about her size. She knew that she was small for her age. Everyone always told her that, but she never had let it get in the way of completing her chores. She always worked as hard as the other children at the State School. Sometimes even harder.

"Won't be long, Grace, and you and Peter'll have your own children. Be nice to have someone help you with the housework and laundry, wouldn't it?"

Grace paused and thought about Myrtle's comment. She might be right. They would probably have a child soon and it would be nice to have an extra set of hands to help with the chores. This child might be small now but would certainly be big enough to help around the house before a baby came along.

"I wasn't comin' here to bring home a child, that's for sure. I didn't even mention it to Peter. Didn't cross our minds, I guess." Grace put her large index finger under Mary's tiny chin. She lifted Mary's chin and turned her head from side to side. "You're not sickly are you? Don't have time for a sickly one around the house, especially with winter coming."

Mary's mouth was dry. She tried to speak, but her tongue was stuck to the roof of her mouth. She licked her lips and swallowed hard.

"No, ma'am. I'm not sickly. I was one of the hardest workers at the orphanage. I promise that I'd work real hard for you, too, if you'd take me home with you, please."

Grace crossed her arms and shifted her weight. "Suppose you might be right, Myrtle. She could be of some help now. I sure didn't plan on bringing an orphan home with me when we left for town this morning. I'm sure Peter wouldn't mind. She sure can't eat more than a bird. What's your name?" Grace asked.

"My name's Mary Sutton," Mary said in a firm and confident voice.

"Mary, huh? Never really liked that name. Too many women named Mary." Grace paused. She looked at the people standing on the train depot platform. She caught the eye of Miss Lewis who was standing near to George. Miss Lewis came over and put her hand on Mary's shoulder.

"Mary was one of our best behaved orphans at the State School Orphanage. I'm sure that you'd enjoy having her as part of your family if you'd take her home today. Won't take long. I have a couple of papers that you need to sign, and she's free to go home with you." Miss Lewis looked at Mary and asked, "Mary, would you like to go home with this woman and be part of her family?"

Mary wasn't quite sure how to answer the question. It would be nice to live in a house again with a mother and a father, but she was a little nervous about Grace Lind. She was intimidating in size and in person. Mary thought about the alternatives. She wasn't sure if the orphan train would stop at more depots along the way or if she would be sent back to the State School. If she wasn't selected this time, she might not get another chance to ride on the orphan train. She was sure, though, that she didn't want to live the rest of her life at the State School. This might be her only opportunity to get a family.

"Yes, I'd like to go home with you, ma'am," Mary uttered nervously. Mary gasped and held her breath for a moment. She thought about what she had said as soon as the words left her lips. It was too late to change her mind.

"All right, give me the papers I need to sign so we can be on our way. Looks like Peter'll be surprised when I come home today."

Miss Lewis handed one paper to Albert and Myrtle Lind and another to Grace. She pointed at the paper and indicated where they needed to sign. George and Mary stood anxiously side by side.

"Hope it's all right if I change her name," Grace said to Miss Lewis. "Never liked the name Mary. Reminds me too much of the Bible. I can think of a better name, I'm sure."

"Yes, you may change her name, Mrs. Lind," Miss Lewis answered politely.

"Good. I'll talk with Peter about it tonight. I'm sure we can think of a name that suits her."

Albert Lind took George by his hand. Myrtle and Grace followed. Mary walked between them. Their horse with a sleigh waited patiently at the front of the depot. Grace hoisted Mary into the sleigh. Albert lifted George. They sat tightly side-by-side on the seat. Myrtle pulled a gray wool blanket over them. Albert guided the horse and sleigh to the main street of Bertha. They stopped at the department store, and Grace purchased new overshoes, mittens, leggings, and a hood for Mary. Albert and Myrtle bought George new clothes, too. Mary and George gazed in wonder at the merchandise in the store. George had never been in a department store. Mary had shopped in the department store in Owatonna with her mother before she died. That made her think about her father and wonder how he was getting along. She doubted that she would ever see him again. How would he ever learn that she had moved north to the small town of Bertha.

They traveled through the open countryside in the horse-drawn sleigh. Mary, George, and Grace sat tightly next to each other. Grace's body helped keep them warm. Mary's new hood and mittens offered protection from the wind, in addition to the wool quilt that covered them.

The gently rolling hills of the prairie were covered with a white blanket of fresh snow that glistened like a million diamonds in the bright sunshine. The storm had ended, and there wasn't a cloud in the brilliant blue sky. A man driving a horse and wagon approached them on the narrow road. Mary peered around Albert so she good get a better look. Albert steered the sleigh to the right side of the road, yelled a firm, "Whoa," to the horses, and pulled back tightly on the leather reins. The sleigh glided to a halt. The man with the wagon pulled alongside.

"Looks like you got that cordwood loaded, Peter," Albert said to his brother.

"Got a full load, so thought I'd sell it in town. Plenty of folks are looking for stove wood for the winter." Peter glanced into the sleigh. "Got a couple extra passengers, I see. Did you pick them up along the way?' he asked.

"We met the orphan train this morning at the depot in Bertha. We picked up a young man to bring home. Should be a big help for me on the farm. There was one little orphan left that no one picked. Guess Grace thought it was time for you to start a family." Albert glanced at Grace, George, and Mary in the sleigh behind him. Peter pulled the wagon forward a few feet. He looked at the three passengers in the sleigh.

"I wasn't planning on bringing home an orphan when I went to town this morning," Grace said to her husband, Peter. She wondered what his reaction was going to be to their new family. "Decided it would be a good idea. We'll have some extra help around the house for when we have our own children."

"What's your name?" Peter said as he looked at Mary.

"My name's Mary, sir. At least that's my name for now. You're wife wants to change it. I'll be fine with whatever name you choose for me."

Peter sat back in the wagon seat. He wasn't expecting that Grace would come home from town with a child, much less one that wasn't afraid to speak up. "Welcome to the family. We can decide on a name for you when I get home. I best get to town with this wood so I can get paid.

Looks like we have another mouth to feed." Peter made a clicking noise, and the horse and full wagon moved slowly. Albert snapped the reins. The sleigh started on the road to George's and Mary's new homes.

Grace showed Mary to her bedroom on the second floor of the small, gray-colored farmhouse. It had a bed with a metal frame and headboard. A multi-colored quilt covered the mattress. There was also a wooden dresser with two drawers. The floors were dark hardwood. Mary unpacked her things from the bag she had brought with her from the orphanage. She laid Lizzie and the black-and-yellow knit scarf on the bed. Mary's faithful companion offered plenty of silent compassion to her over the years.

Mary's room had a view of the red barn and farmyard. There were several black-and-white dairy cows, a few pigs, and a faded red chicken coop at the side of the barn. Most of the birds were inside the coop, out of the cold weather. A big yellow dog chased a black-and-white cat. The cat slid quickly under the barn door out of the dog's reach. Mary was looking forward to having pets, especially a dog. Pets weren't allowed at the State School, although there were some stray cats that helped contain the mouse population in the barns. Mary watched Grace walk through the yard and to the barn. She yelled something to the dog and shooed it away from the barn door. The dog was eager to get another chance at the black-and-white cat, but Grace didn't allow him the opportunity. She closed the barn door behind her.

Mary and Grace waited for Peter to return from town. Mary wasn't exactly sure what she was supposed to do so she waited patiently for Grace to give her instructions. They prepared dinner. Mary helped as much as she could. "You can set the dishes on the table for dinner. The plates are in the cupboard on this side of the kitchen. There's a small stepstool in the corner if you can't reach. Are you sure that you're eight years old? I don't believe it. I don't think you can even look over the dining room table, child."

Mary didn't respond to Grace's comment about her size. She was accustomed to hearing that she was small for her age.

"Did you hear what I said? Are you really eight years old?" Grace asked.

Mary hadn't thought that Grace was really looking for an answer to her question. She realized that she better answer when Grace barked the question a second time.

"Yes, ma'am. I'm eight years old. I was born May 17, 1898."

Mary carefully set the dishes on the table. She put a place setting of silverware next to each plate. She went back to the kitchen to get more directions from Grace. Just then, Peter walked into the kitchen. Grace gave him instructions to wash up. Dinner would be ready soon.

Mary and Grace cleared the table and did the dishes after dinner. Peter did chores in the barn. They all settled in the parlor when all the work was done. A stone fireplace warmed the room.

Mary was happy that Myrtle Lind had encouraged Grace to take an orphan from the train. Mary shuddered at the thought of returning to the orphanage on the orphan train. How awful it would have felt not to be chosen. How terrible it was not to be wanted. She remembered how unwanted she felt as she stood on the platform and hoped to be selected.

Grace and Peter talked about the events of the day. Grace thought of new names for Mary. She offered her suggestions to Peter. Either her suggestions didn't appeal to Peter, or he wasn't listening to her. "I think we should name her Marjorie. What do you think of the name Marjorie, Peter? Do you think she looks like a Marjorie?"

"Grace, I think her name, Mary, is a fine name, but if you want to change her name to Marjorie, it's all right with me. Whatever you like," Peter said with a tired sigh.

Mary didn't understand why she couldn't keep her name. And, why did they have to decide on a name today? Couldn't it wait? Mary was tired and looking forward to going to bed. The events of the day had worn her down. She didn't feel like she had a single bit of energy left in her tiny body. She wondered how she was going to walk up the stairs to bed.

"Mary . . . I mean Marjorie," Peter said. "You look tired. You've had a long day. Why don't you come over here and sit on my lap a bit." Mary slid off the couch and walked apprehensively to Peter. She kept an eye on Grace the whole time, however. It seemed that most of the direction in the family came from her. She didn't appear to be the kind of person that you'd want to cross. Peter, however, seemed more warm and friendly.

Peter opened his arms, and Marjorie climbed onto his lap. "You've had a long day, little girl. He rested her head on his shoulder with his hand. "What do you think of your new name? Do you like Marjorie?"

Mary thought for a moment. Tears started to well in her eyes. "It's a fine name, sir." Mary answered.

"How 'bout if you call us Mom and Dad, Marjorie? Do you think you can do that?"

Mary was too choked with tears to speak. She nodded her head instead. Mom and Dad, she thought, a family at last. She silently hoped that this family would last for a long time. She rested her head on Peter's shoulder and softly cried herself to sleep.

ॐ 17 ॐ

G RACE AND PETER LIND'S FIRST CHILD, CONSOLO, arrived on February 29, 1908. She was a cute little baby, and she resembled her father. Marjorie's responsibilities included caring for Consolo, in addition to her other daily chores. The Lind family grew again on November 6, 1910, with the addition of a baby boy, Darwin, which added more to Marjorie's duties. Shortly after Darwin's birth, Consolo died. Grace found the lifeless baby in her bed early one morning. Consolo had stopped breathing in her sleep.

Marjorie did whatever she could to help Grace. The harder she worked, however, the more Grace wanted her to do, or she expressed her displeasure with what Marjorie had done.

Marjorie attended a small country school about one and one-half miles from the Lind's farm. She loved to go to school. She especially enjoyed reading. Grace made a clear distinction between school and home—school was where school work was done, and home was where chores were done. The two didn't overlap. Marjorie worked as hard as she could on evenings and weekends so that she could go to school.

Grace didn't allow Marjorie to bring books home from school. Sometimes she sneaked books home from school, though, so that she

Marjorie's class at school.

could read them in the evening in her bedroom after her chores were done. Marjorie would leave the school books in the ditch outside the house. She'd wait for it to get dark outside and then sneak outside when she was sure no one was watching. She read the books by candlelight in her bedroom. She didn't dare stay up too late and burn too much of the candle or Grace would figure out what she was doing. Marjorie put the books back in the ditch late at night or very early morning and collected them on her way back to school. She always said a small prayer that Grace wouldn't catch her. Surely Grace would severely discipline her for what she had done.

Grace was always swift to let Marjorie know when her work wasn't up to her standards or completed on time. Marjorie suffered several incidents of Grace's abusive and cruel discipline. One incident occurred when Marjorie, who was nine years old, was helping Grace make butter. Grace churned the butter with her muscular arms. She churned slower and slower as the butter thickened. Marjorie scooped the yellow butter from the churn and placed it on a tray on the counter. They kept an open kettle of boiling water on the stove that Marjorie used to warm a metal spoon to cut through the solid butter in the churn. Inadvertently, Marjorie left the spoon in the kettle of boiling water for a short time. The metal spoon handle was very hot the next time she touched it. Marjorie immediately dropped the hot spoon, and it fell to the bottom of the kettle of boiling water. Marjorie quickly jumped back from the boiling kettle. She blew on her burned fingers. She waved her hand in the air but was unsuccessful in easing the pain. She tried to cool her fingers in her mouth.

Grace witnessed the incident and instantly told Marjorie how stupid she was—of course, the spoon handle would be hot. Grace grabbed Marjorie by her shoulder. She brought Marjorie close to the stove and screamed at her. "Burned your hand, huh? You should've known that handle was hot. How stupid can you be?" Grace dug her strong fingers hard into Marjorie's shoulder. "I'll teach you not to do that again. You think your fingers hurt, now? I'll give you some pain that you'll never forget. You'll never do that again. Put your hand in the kettle and get the spoon for me."

Marjorie was terrified. She wasn't about to put her hand in a kettle of actively boiling water. The warm spoon handle had already put a large red burn on her fingertips and the palm of her hand. Grace shook Marjorie again. Grace swatted Marjorie on the back of her head so hard with her big open hand that she must have felt like she was hit by a large board. Marjorie nearly lost her balance from Grace's strong blow. "Did you hear me, you stupid orphan?"

Marjorie hated it when Grace called her an orphan. It was a stigma that she wore with her at school and in the community. That was bad enough. She didn't need to hear the same cruel remarks at home from her mother, too; but it was Grace's common remark to Marjorie when she was angry. Peter was much more even-tempered. He raised his voice at times but he never abused Marjorie, physically or verbally, as

Grace did. "I want you to reach in that kettle this instant and get that spoon for me. If not, I'll pour the whole pot over you."

Marjorie shook in fright. Perhaps, if she was able to grab the spoon quickly from the bottom of the kettle it would only burn her hand a little. It certainly wouldn't be as bad as if she had the entire kettle of water poured on her body. Grace towered over Marjorie. "Now!" Grace screamed.

Marjorie reached into the kettle. Her scream of pain pierced the air when her hand touched the boiling water. She retrieved the spoon and immediately dropped it on the floor. Tears swelled in her eyes. Marjorie grabbed her burned right hand with her left hand and cradled it next to her body. Almost immediately, large water blisters formed. Screaming in pain, Marjorie ran out of the house to the backyard. She submerged her burning hand into a trough of water. It felt like her entire hand, up to her wrist, was on fire. The pain dissipated but only for a moment. She found a soft cloth in the bottom of the wicker clothes basket near the laundry lines. Carefully, she wrapped her blistered hand to keep it out of the air. Slowly, hunched over in pain, Marjorie walked to the other side of the house and sat on the grass under a large willow tree. She tried to hide her tears. She tried to hide the hurt that pierced her so deeply. It was hard to tell what Grace would do to her if she caught her crying.

Marjorie thought about the unspeakable horror of Grace's rages of anger. Maybe she should leave. Where could she go? Staying or running away were equally as dangerous. Maybe she should tell someone. But whom would she tell? From what she knew, it seemed like a way of life for an orphan. There was no hope.

Most of the orphans weren't treated as family members. Although the Linds changed Marjorie's last name to Lind, they never legally adopted her. Usually the orphans provided additional labor on the farm or became nannies. Seldom were the orphans adopted, rather they were indentured for labor. Conveniently, Grace and Peter Lind took Marjorie into their home before they started their family. That became obvious to Marjorie as soon as Consolo was born.

Marjorie wondered what would happen to her if she told some-one about Grace's abuse. Surely she wouldn't be able to live with the Linds any longer. Grace would make her life a living hell on earth. Perhaps they would send her back to the State School Orphanage. Marjorie remembered her life of routine and lack of freedom at the State School in Owatonna. At least she had a bit more independence at the Linds. Marjorie decided that the cruel conditions of her life with the Linds needed to remain a carefully guarded secret. She was afraid that if anyone found out, they would send her back to the stringent life at the orphanage.

Marjorie went to school the next day with her hand wrapped in a soft white cloth. It was hard for her to hide the large bandage from her teacher and her classmates. Everyone was curious about how she hurt her hand. She knew that she couldn't tell them the truth so she made up a story about how she bumped the handle of a kettle of boil-ing water on the stove. The kettle tipped, and the boiling water poured over her hand. Her classmates asked to see her hand but she kept it hid-den as best and as long as she could. Eventually, the blisters popped and the skin dried. New, bright pink skin formed under the old. She hated lying to her classmates but knew that she had to keep her secret safe or face Grace's revenge or, even worse, be sent back to the orphanage.

Marjorie continued to advance a grade at school every year, as time went on. She studied hard while at school. She liked learning new things and also especially enjoyed the company of the other students.

The Lind's third child, Ross, was born on July 2, 1914. Ross developed horrific canker sores on the inside of his mouth soon after his birth. The inside of his mouth was covered with shallow red sores. The doctor thought that the condition was perhaps related to an allergy to milk. The sores caused Ross such pain that he cried continuously. It was nearly impossible for him to eat. Ross died twenty-four days after his birth.

Occasionally, as a special treat, Grace and Peter allowed Marjorie the opportunity to visit her cousins, Virgil, Alice, and Hope

Lind. They lived on the adjacent farm property. Both families attended the German Lutheran Church in east Bertha and frequently saw each other on Sundays. In 1915 her cousins began a series of confirmation classes at the church. Marjorie pleaded with Grace and Peter because she wanted to attend, too. The classes started at the church in the early fall. If the students successfully completed all the lessons over several months, they would be confirmed at a special ceremony at church on Easter Sunday. Faithfully, Marjorie attended the confirmation classes. Once a week, she walked to Uncle Albert and Aunt Myrtle's house. Cousins Virgil, Alice, and Hope joined her for a walk to Louis Smith's house where the classes were held. They were met by four other confirmation students and Reverend Role, who taught the classes. Marjorie found the teachings very fascinating. She couldn't wait for the day when she would finally be confirmed in her faith.

Easter Sunday arrived late in April 1916. Marjorie eagerly anticipated her big day for months. She even planned what she was going to wear. One of her cousins gave her a special dress that she had outgrown. It was aqua-marine blue, her favorite color. It made her bright blue eyes shine like brilliant jewels. The dress fit her perfectly and was much more stylish than the dull hand-me-down house dresses she usually wore.

At dinner on Saturday evening, Marjorie told Grace and Peter about how excited she was for her big day at church the next day. There were twelve students in all to be confirmed in their faith. "I can't wait for tomorrow. I'm really looking forward to going to Easter services. Alice and I talked at school about it yesterday. Reverend Role is going to have a special church service for our confirmation. We get to sit in the front pews of the church. He's going to recognize us for our studies over the last months." Marjorie was proud of her accomplishments and couldn't wait to be recognized along with her peers.

Neither Peter nor Grace acknowledged what she was saying. Darwin looked up from his plate. "Will I have to take these classes, too, some day?" Darwin asked. "Sounds like a lot of extra reading and studying to me. I get my fill of that type of work at school," he added.

"Sounds like a bunch of nonsense to me, Darwin," Peter said. "You have enough work to do on the farm to keep you busy. You can pray while you work if you want. No need to take classes to learn how to say a prayer. Makes no sense to me at all."

Marjorie listened quietly to their conversation. She didn't agree with Peter's comments but most certainly didn't want to correct him. She learned so much about her faith and the teachings in the Bible. The classes weren't about memorizing prayers. She could say her own prayers. She didn't need to recite a prayer that someone else had written.

"You know, Darwin, I think your father's right. You won't be going to confirmation classes. You're right, Peter, those confirmation classes are a bunch of nonsense. I don't know why Albert and Myrtle let their kids go to these classes. Just a waste of time if you ask me." Grace went back to her meal.

Darwin breathed a heavy sigh of relief. He stood up and pushed his chair under the table and made a quick exit outside before his parents could change their minds. Marjorie listened to Grace and Peter's conversation. She wanted to tell them what she learned by reading the Bible and discussing the readings with the other students and Reverend Role. She believed in the teachings in the Bible and wanted to be confirmed in her faith. Silently, she cleared the dishes as Peter left the table.

"Got to finish chores. Too much work to be done to waste time talking about the Bible. Do enough of that on Sunday if you ask me," Peter said as he walked through the kitchen and to the back door.

"You're right about the work around here, Peter. Too much to be done, especially with spring planting and the new calves. Probably best if we don't go to church tomorrow. Can get more done around here, and I'm sure it won't matter to God. He'll still treat us the same one way or the other."

Marjorie's mouth dropped open. She couldn't believe what she just heard. "I have to go church tomorrow. It's my confirmation day."

"You heard what your father said. Too much work to do around here. You can help him and Darwin with the planting. Looks like the weather is going to cooperate, too. Should be a perfect day for planting. I'm sure they can use an extra hand. Earn your keep for once. That's why we took you off the orphan train in the first place."

Marjorie had heard Grace's cruel words so many times before. Her words usually fell on deaf ears. "Please, please, may I go to church tomorrow?" Mary begged. "It's such an important day for me. I studied hard and learned all my lessons. I want to be confirmed with the others in the class. The service will only be an hour. I promise I'll run home afterwards. You'll hardly know that I was gone," Marjorie pleaded.

Grace's word was always final. It didn't make much sense to beg her. Once Grace made up her mind, right or wrong, she wouldn't change. Marjorie could tell that Grace had dug her heels in hard on the matter of her confirmation.

Marjorie was stunned. She felt like life itself had been sucked from her body. She couldn't believe that Grace wasn't going to allow her to attend confirmation. Maybe she was dreaming. Perhaps she would wake up in a few minutes and find out that she was just having a bad dream. Maybe she would ignore Grace. She thought about the brutal consequences and decided that disobeying Grace wasn't an option.

Marjorie's dreams of her confirmation day were crushed with painful disappointment. She tried hard not to show her discontent. It would only give Grace more reason to retaliate. She washed and dried the dishes in silence. She couldn't wait to leave the kitchen. She wanted to get as much distance as she could from Grace.

Marjorie went into the yard after her evening chores were done. She wanted to be alone and have some time to think. The sun was setting on the sweet spring landscape, and a bright red glow filled the sky as the golden sun dropped lower and lower. A robin sang an evening song from a branch in the big willow tree. Marjorie closed her eyes and took a deep breath. It felt good to fill her lungs with the fresh spring air. Slowly she let out the air. She took another deep breath. It helped to clear her head. Marjorie untied her dingy white apron, slipped it off, and threw it over her shoulder. As she walked on the narrow cow path to a small pond in the pasture she noticed that the grass was starting to peek through the barren earth on the sides of the path. Marjorie gathered a few crumbs of comfort when she picked up a pebble and threw it into the water. She wanted to lash out at Grace but what good would it do? It would only feel good for the moment. It would only come back to haunt her. Each day with Grace was becoming more unpredictable, and the events of the last couple hours refused to leave her mind. Marjorie watched the rings grow in the calm water. Each ring was larger than the next. Eventually they disappeared. She threw another pebble. The rings grew and disappeared again. The only way she could imagine to rid herself of Grace's repression was to leave and begin a life of her own. In a few weeks she would celebrate her eighteenth birthday. It was time. Grace had dealt her last blow. Like the rings in the water, it was time for her to expand, move on. She needed to make a plan.

❧ 18 ❧

S OLD," THE AUCTIONEER YELLED AS HE pounded his gavel on a wood-en table. "Sold to the man in the red plaid jacket."

Grace's parents, William and Nellie Talmadge had sold their farm to Clarence Fox a few weeks before. The farm was too much work for them. Grace's mother suffered from severe arthritis in her joints, and it was difficult for her to walk. Grace's father couldn't do all the work on the farm by himself any longer. They bought a small house on the outskirts of Bertha and decided to sell their farm equipment and many household items at an auction.

Marjorie went to Grandma and Grandpa Talmadge's farm in mid-October to help them prepare for the auction and get settled in their new house. At first, her plan was to stay with Grandma and Grandpa until they were settled in their new place. The Talmadges were grateful to Marjorie and the help she offered them. The longer she stayed, the more Marjorie knew that she would never go back to live with Grace and Peter Lind.

Marjorie enjoyed living with Grandma and Grandpa Talmadge. They were kind people. They appreciated Marjorie and paid her a small wage for her work. Marjorie couldn't understand why Grace, their daughter, was such a hard and angry person. Her parents were just the opposite.

Grandma Talmadge taught Marjorie how to sew and embroider. Together, they made curtains for the new house. In the evening, they sat in the parlor and enjoyed each other's company while they worked on needlework projects.

The time flew by. Marjorie saved most of the money that Grandma and Grandpa paid her. One day, at the general store in town, Marjorie talked to Mrs. Meyer. They knew each other from church. Mrs. Meyer was happy to see that Marjorie was doing well. She asked her about her plans for the future. Marjorie knew that it was time for her to start a life of her own. She wasn't exactly sure what she would do, however, if she left the small town of Bertha. She hadn't traveled outside of the town's limits since she arrived more than a dozen years before.

"I went to visit my sister in Long Prairie recently. It's just a short train ride from here. It's a bigger town than Bertha, and it's growing. It's the county seat of Todd County," Mrs. Meyer told Marjorie.

"What kind of work do you think that I could find? I don't have any training, other than housework. I'm a hard worker. I suppose there are always people looking for an extra hand around the house."

"I'm sure you wouldn't have a problem finding work in Long Prairie, Marjorie. The town's growing so fast. Think about it, Marjorie. You have a full life ahead of you. If you're interested, I'll write my sister and ask her if you can stay with her for a time while you look for work."

"Oh, Mrs. Meyer, it's kind of you to offer. I've saved some money since I've been living with Grandma and Grandpa. It's the first money that I've ever had. I'm sure that I have enough for a train ticket. I'll think about your offer. I want to talk to Grandma and Grandpa before I decide to leave. They'll need to find someone to help them around the house if I'm not there."

The thought of moving was exciting and scary at the same time. Hundreds of thoughts and questions screamed through Marjorie's head all at once. Mrs. Meyer had presented her with a wonderful opportunity. It might be the opportunity of a lifetime. She might never have this chance again. She worried about what Grandma and Grandpa would say. They depended on her for many of the chores around the house, and she didn't want to disappoint them. She hoped they would be able to find someone to replace her. "I'll talk to Grandma and Grandpa in the next couple days, Mrs. Meyer. How 'bout if I let you know what they say when I see you at church services on Sunday."

"Sounds like a good idea to me. The Talmadges have been very nice to you, haven't they? I know they need your help, and I appreciate your concern. You're very thoughtful, Marjorie. I'll see you on Sunday. Give my best to Mr. and Mrs. Talmadge."

Marjorie walked home with her packages. She thought carefully about what she would say to Grandma and Grandpa. She hated to leave them. They had been so kind to her, but it was time to get out on her own, time for her to start a life of her own.

ை 19 ஐ

"ALL ABOARD! ALL ABOARD," THE CONDUCTOR called from the platform at the front of the small train depot in Bertha. His breath
billowed from his lips in small, puffy clouds as he called again,
"All aboard!" The air was cold. It was December 10, 1917.

About a month earlier, Grace gave birth to Marcella Lind, Grace
and Peter's last child. Marjorie had only seen their new baby a few times
since she lived with Grandma and Grandpa Talmadge. She offered to come
back home and help Grace with the new baby, but Grace told Marjorie that
she didn't want her help and that she should stay with Grandma and
Grandpa. She didn't want Marjorie ever to come back. Marjorie always
liked Peter better than Grace. She could be so stubborn and crabby.

Passengers said good-bye to friends and relatives on the platform. Other passengers had already boarded the train and were out of
the bitter winter wind. They waved good-bye through the frosty train
window. "Looks like I best get on board before that train decides to
leave without me." Marjorie was nervous and excited at the same time.
Peter and Darwin came to the depot to see her off.

"Have a good trip, Marjorie." Peter hunched his shoulders and
turned his coat collar up to protect his neck from the cold wind. "Will

Marjorie at age eighteen.

you write and let us know where you end up? We hope everything works out for you."

Darwin held out his right hand to Marjorie. "Good luck, Marjorie. Come back and see us sometime, if you can."

"I appreciate your coming to see me off, Dad and Darwin. Thank you for coming." The train whistle sounded. It echoed through the clear air. "Guess I better get on board," she said with a crack in her voice. "Would you please give my best to Mom? I would have come home to say good-bye, but I thought she might come to the depot to see me off. Say good-bye for me."

Peter and Darwin nodded their heads in unison. Neither commented on why Grace wasn't at the depot. They didn't know exactly what to say. It was better left unsaid.

Marjorie boarded the train. She carried all her possessions with her in a small travel bag that she had bought with the money she earned. She smiled and waved a final good-bye to Peter and Darwin through the frosty train window. Marjorie put her bag on the train floor. It protected her feet from the cool breeze there. She took off her hat and set it on her lap with a sigh of relief.

It was a little over eleven years before that she had arrived at the same train depot in Bertha on the orphan train. She remembered the excitement of that day. She remembered it well. How lucky she felt when Grace Lind selected her from the depot platform. She felt fortunate that she didn't have to return to the State School Orphanage in Owatonna. Lonely and frightened, she sat on Peter's lap and cried herself to sleep the first night in her new home.

Hundreds of memories traveled with her as the train rolled down the track. Bertha disappeared in the distance. Marjorie rested her head on the back of her seat. She watched the countryside whisk by while she looked out the train window. A single tear of relief rolled down her cheek. She closed her eyes and whispered a prayer to herself. She prayed that God would watch over her and keep her safe as she traveled to her unknown future.

MARJORIE SETTLED QUICKLY IN LONG PRAIRIE, a town located in the geographical center of Minnesota and named in 1867 for its rolling prairie grasslands. It was home to the Todd County Courthouse and jail.

Marjorie landed a job as a maid for Mr. and Mrs. Losey on Lake Street almost immediately. They weren't wealthy people, but they certainly had enough to get by on. Mr. Losey worked in the grocery department of Hart's store. Mrs. Losey worked at the candy counter. They had three boys, Richard, LeRoy, and Claud. Marjorie's starting wage was three dollars and fifty cents per week, a very modest salary, but the Loseys gave her free room and board, and that helped with her living.

The small town was surrounded by rich farmland. The Long Prairie River stretched through the county. It was one of a few rivers, like the Red River, in the State of Minnesota that flowed from the south to the north.

Marjorie often did housework for other families in town as her time permitted. She was quick to make friends with Ella Bliese, the housekeeper for Mr. and Mrs. Hart, owners of the town's department store. They met while attending services at the Long Prairie United Methodist Church. They enjoyed each other's company and frequently, on Sunday afternoons, took long walks into the picturesque country-side. It was their only day off work during the week. Pristine water in the ponds and small lakes glistened in the bright mid-day sunshine. Marjorie couldn't resist the temptation of the fresh spring air. It was her favorite time of the year. Ella and Marjorie talked about the past and the future as they walked.

One Sunday in May, Marjorie and Ella were standing on a small wooden bridge over the Long Prairie River when along came a car with two young men. The small overpass bounced and shook as the car drove onto the bridge. Marjorie and Ella quickly moved out of the way of the fast approaching car, which was driven by a young man wearing a sporty looking brown cap. His companion poked his head out of the car window as it came to a sudden stop a few feet in front of where Marjorie and Ella stood. Very politely, the young man introduced himself as Frank Renn. The driver leaned over Frank toward the window. He grinned and said, "Hello, girls! My name's George Peterson. You girls want to go for a ride with us? We're not heading anywhere in particular, just out enjoying this beautiful day."

Marjorie and Ella looked at each other with excitement and graciously accepted. Frank opened the back door of the black car, and they slid across the car's dusty back seat. Marjorie, Ella, George, and Frank spent the pleasant spring afternoon touring the countryside. They enjoyed the scenery and soaked up the bright spring sunshine while they rode on bumpy dirt roads. Freezing winter temperatures followed by warm weather and rainstorms usually made the roads uneven and rough. A trail of dust followed them on the narrow, uneven paths.

The automobile was growing more popular, becoming an increasingly more important part of American lives. It helped increase productivity and efficiency, which allowed families more free time. It also provided a perfect means for young people to socialize and have fun. The three hundred fifty dollar price tag for a new Model T, however, usually put the automobile out of the affordable range for most families.

Late in the afternoon, George asked Marjorie and Ella if they'd like to join him and Frank at his parents' house for dinner. Marjorie and Ella were thrilled at the opportunity and jumped at the chance. They were excited to spend more time with the debonair young men that happened upon them earlier in the day.

George was a very tall and slender man. The top of Marjorie's head barely reached to his underarm. He had sandy brown hair with a light-reddish tint. Like many Norwegians, George's father immigrated to the United States. The climate and terrain in Minnesota was very similar to his homeland, so he and his wife decided to make Minnesota their new home.

George was soft spoken and a little shy. He didn't say too much. As he walked Marjorie home after dinner, George asked if she would like to go for a car ride again the next Sunday. Marjorie graciously accepted. She was excited about her new-found beau. The anticipation of their next date gave her something to look forward to throughout the coming week.

After a short courtship, Marjorie and George married on December 10, 1919. It was exactly two years from the date that Marjorie took the train from Bertha and made her home in Long Prairie. Everett Peterson, George's cousin, was his best man. Alice Lind, Marjorie's cousin, was her bridesmaid. She wore a Copenhagen blue wool dress she had made herself.

George and Marjorie went on a short honeymoon to Bertha. Marjorie wasn't interested in showing her new husband off to Peter and Grace, so they stayed with Uncle Albert and Aunt Myrtle for a couple days. Marjorie enjoyed their company, but even more she enjoyed the opportunity to catch up with her cousins. It was hard to believe that it had been two years since she had seen them. So much had happened in those years.

After the wedding, George and Marjorie moved to Reynolds Township near Long Prairie. They lived with George's brother, Hiram, and his wife, Ellen, in the upper level of their farm house. George

George and Marjorie's wedding.

helped Hiram plant and harvest the crops. Marjorie worked with Ellen in the garden and helped with the housework.

George and Hiram built a small house on the farmland. George and Marjorie moved into the new house on New Years Day 1921.

In April 1922, Hiram and Ellen moved in with George's mother in her house in Long Prairie, shortly after the birth of Harlan, their only child. George and Marjorie moved into Hiram and Ellen's house and continued to farm the land. They added some milk cows and chickens.

On February 2, 1923, Marjorie gave birth to Shirley, the first of their seven children. There was a blinding blizzard that evening. Dr. VanValkenberg, with the help of his driver, Shorty Russell, arrived in the nick of time to deliver the baby.

Their second child, Myrtle, was born on July 29, 1925. When Myrtle was two weeks old, George went to North Dakota to work. The substantial wage that he could earn in the harvest fields was an opportunity he couldn't pass up; however it meant leaving Marjorie alone on the farm with two infant children. Marjorie milked the cows and took care of the chickens. She canned peas, corn, and beans from the large vegetable garden she tended. The canned food would help feed their growing family in the long winter months. Hiram came to the farm and helped with the crops until George returned.

Life as most Americans knew it changed in the mid-1920s. The use of machinery on farms increased productivity. Most small farmers, like Marjorie and George, lacked the capital to purchase it. The industrial boom drew laborers off the farms to factories in the cities. Demand for food, however, remained constant. As a result, food prices dropped. Small farmers found it more and more difficult to compete and sold out to larger farmers.

Like many small farmers, Marjorie and George left the farm. They rented their farm land to another farmer and moved to town on the west side of Long Prairie. It was March 1926, George worked for the Dray Company, a freight shipping company. He unloaded freight from train cars at the rail yard. In the winter months, he cut cordwood to supplement their income. They took a couple roomers into their modest house, including George's mother, who was widowed and growing older.

George and Marjorie's third daughter, Betty, was born on May 4, 1927. Two weeks later they moved to a different house on the west side of Long Prairie. They called it the "brown house." The house earned the name from the house's lack of paint, not from the color of its exterior. They lived in the brown house for eleven years.

ഞ 20 ൙

THE STOCK MARKET CRASH OF 1929 ushered in the Great Depression. Banks failed. The highly prosperous economic times that brought updates, such as the radio and the washing machine to America's homes in the 1920s, came to a screeching halt. Unemployment skyrocketed. Franklin Roosevelt was elected president in 1933. He proposed the New Deal, a program intended to stimulate and revitalize the economy. The program used government money to combat large-scale unemployment and severely negative economic growth.

Marjorie and George's fourth daughter, Hazel, was born on February 15, 1931. It was difficult for George to find work, despite the government intervention implemented by President Roosevelt. George worked as a hired hand on farms and did planting and threshing. He worked other odd jobs when he could find them. Money was tight, especially with four growing children.

Then, to add insult to injury, severe drought moved from the East Coast of the United States, through the Midwest, and into the Great Plains states. The massive drought began in 1930 and lasted until 1941. The era was well-known as the Dust Bowl or the "Dirty Thirties."

Strong dust storms in 1933 removed massive amounts of topsoil from desiccated farmland. Crops planted in the spring that year shriveled in the intense heat and dropped to the ground. There was nothing for the farmers to harvest. There was no harvest work for George on the farms that fall. Marjorie and George's first son, Gerald, was born on June 30 that year.

Unable to find work, George and Marjorie traveled north in the state for a few days. They heard that blueberries in the northern woods were flourishing in the warm weather and arid conditions. They camped along the way, took food along, and had a gas camp stove to cook on. In a couple of days, they filled their two-wheel trailer full of blueberries, took them home and sold them—two quarts for twenty-five cents. The money they made helped with their living that summer.

The year 1936 was Marjorie and George's worst year. In May that year George took sick. He had a growth on his neck. The side of his neck below his ear was swollen and very sore to the touch. The doctor in Long Prairie was unable to diagnose the condition. He made an appointment for George with a specialist at the University of Minnesota Hospital in Minneapolis. University doctors had the latest research equipment and performed advanced medical tests in their research facilities. George traveled to Minneapolis several times. The university was about one hundred twenty-five miles from Long Prairie.

At first, George's unusual medical condition baffled the doctors. After a long series of tests, the doctors diagnosed George's illness as tuberculosis. Active tuberculosis was highly contagious and spread quickly from one person to another through inhalation. A cough or sneeze was all that was needed to spread the deadly disease. The bacteria usually settled in the lungs and began to grow. From there, the infection moved steadily through the blood to other parts of the body, such as the spine, kidneys, or brain. The condition was also known as consumption, for its all-consuming nature on the human body. Tuberculosis had an enormous impact on the health of many people, rich and poor. It was the cause of death for thousands.

Complete isolation from other people was required to help stop the spread of the potentially deadly disease. Treatment of tuberculosis included heavy doses of antibiotics and vitamins and several months of bed rest. Sanitariums—tuberculosis hospitals—offered patients a restful place to recuperate and sprang up in communities of all sizes.

In September 1936, George went to the Wadena Sanitarium, about forty miles from Long Prairie for rest and treatment. Marjorie had just given birth to Marvin, their second son. Marvin was only three weeks old. She was thankful that she hadn't contracted tuberculosis during her pregnancy. None of the other children were sick either. Marjorie wasn't sure when George would return home, as treatment could take anywhere from a few months to years, if he returned at all. His recuperation depended on how he responded to the treatment and rest. Many people never recovered from the disease. They died in the sanitarium.

Marjorie worried about how she was going to make it on her own with six young children. George was the sole breadwinner. Shirley, Myrtle, and Betty, the oldest of the children, helped out when they could. They babysat for other families and occasionally cleaned houses on weekends. Their modest income offered little economic relief for the family. Marjorie had no choice. She applied for a Mother's Pension, a public aid program for single mothers who were the sole support of dependent children. Deserving mothers who were temporarily without the support of the family breadwinner could apply for Minnesota state funds. The public cash assistance program was designed to keep children in their homes to be reared by their parents rather than in public institutions such as orphanages.

The amount of funds that a single mother received was based on the number of children in the family. Marjorie received forty dollars per month from the pension to support her family of six children. She was grateful for the monthly payment she received, but it wasn't nearly enough to support the family. She tried to find work. Unable to do so, she did washing and ironing for others in her home.

George recuperated at the Wadena Sanitarium for two months. He returned home for Thanksgiving but wasn't able to work for a year. Marjorie continued to take laundry into their home, and she also tended a very large garden which helped with her family's living. Sometimes she sold her vegetables. Finally, in the spring of 1937 George was able to work again. He found work on area farms doing planting while he also cleared land for farmers and sold cordwood.

September 20, 1938, George and Marjorie's seventh and last child, a boy, Elwin, was born.

ഔ 21 ര

THE LIGHT IN MARJORIE'S SEWING ROOM FLICKED ON. The bright light from the clear, cut-glass fixture in the bedroom ceiling broke the darkness and cast interestingly shaped shadows around the room. The light surprised Ann, and she sat up straight. "Oh, Mom," she said breathlessly as she stared at her mother. "You startled me." Betty was standing in the doorway to the bedroom. Ann took a deep breath and let it out slowly. She rested the small, gray cardboard-covered book that she was reading on her lap.

Betty walked into the bedroom. "Earth to Ann," Betty sang as she touched Ann gently on the shoulder and shook her. "I called your name twice from the doorway, and you didn't answer. I thought maybe I could get your attention if I turned on the light. Don't you think it's a little dark to be reading in here anyway?'

Ann looked out the small bedroom window. It was dusk. The big shade trees in the yard cast long shadows on the lawn. "I didn't realize that it was so late. What time is it?" Ann asked.

"It's almost 8:45. I think it's about time for you to come out of this room. Are you still reading Mom's autobiography?" Betty questioned.

"Oh, Mom, I couldn't put it down. What a fascinating account she wrote about her life. I didn't know anything about most of the events she wrote about." Ann quickly fired off a litany of questions, one after the other. She didn't pause long enough to allow her mother the opportunity to respond. "How in the world did she make it? Where did she find the strength to survive? Why do you think she stayed with the Linds? Do you wonder if she ever thought about running away? She was one heck of a resilient child and an even stronger and more courageous woman." Ann rubbed her hand on the cover of Marjorie's autobiography. She fingered the cording that held the pages of the book together. "Did you know, Mom, by the time Grandma was eight years old that she had lived in five different places and had two different names? Her first name was Mary when she was adopted by the Philip and Josephine Sutton. The Linds changed her first name to Marjorie when they took her off the orphan train and into their home. She took the Linds' last name, even though they never formally adopted her." Ann talked faster the longer she talked. She always delivered her words quickly when she was trying to make a point. "Can you imagine, Mom? If she was a child in this day and age, and she faced the circumstances and the changes that she did—heck, she'd be in therapy for the rest of her life."

Betty listened carefully as Ann spoke. She thought about her mother. She thought about what her mother's life must have been like when she was a child.

"Mom, why do you think that Grandma never talked about her life? She never talked about her past. She never mentioned any of the things she wrote in this book." Ann held the small cardboard covered book in her hand.

Betty said thoughtfully, "I don't think your grandma ever thought her life was much different from anyone else's. There were some very hard years for everyone, especially during the Depression. Times were tough, really tough. Everyone faced the same conditions, the same failing economy. Jobs were scarce, and wages were small, if you were even able to find work. You had to make do with what you had. It was just the way that it was." Betty paused and thought for a few moments. With a slight smile and a light chuckle she said, "I don't think we knew that we were poor. It was just the way it was."

"Why do you think Grandma wrote her autobiography? Why was it important for her to write her story?" Ann asked.

"Grandma was a very modest and humble person. You know that. Rarely did she ever talk about herself, unless, of course, you asked her. I think in hindsight, in her later years, she realized that she had traveled a remarkable journey through life. I think she was proud of who she was. She was a survivor. She made it."

"What an understatement. I was always proud of Grandma. But I have even more admiration for her after reading her life story. The world challenged her almost every single step of her life. She never let anything get her down. She let adversity bounce right off her. And, in spite of it all, she was the kindest and gentlest woman. She looked for ways to give back to the world that challenged her. She was always looking for opportunities to give to people less fortunate than she was. What a woman!"

"You're absolutely right, Ann. She was quite the woman. We can learn so much from her. We should try to live in her image."

Ann raised her eyebrows and shook her head from side to side. "I'll sure try, but I'll never hold a candle to her."

"I think there's a second reason why Mom wrote her story," Betty said with slow deliberation. She thought carefully for a moment. "I think she wanted her story to live on, especially within our family."

"Absolutely," Ann said quickly. "I agree wholeheartedly. Everyone in our family should read this. They should share it with their families. That way Grandma can live on forever in our family. In a couple weeks, when things settle down, after the funeral, I'll make copies of Grandma's autobiography and share it with the family. I'll include a digital copy with each hardcopy." Ann carefully placed Marjorie's autobiography on the night stand next to the bed. She stared at Marjorie's handwriting on the front cover—"My Autobiography, My Life— Marjorie Peterson."—a simple title for the story of a very rich life.

"I'm sure everyone in the family would be grateful to have a copy. You're right, she would live on forever." Betty patted Ann on the back and motioned to the door. "It's time for us leave for the evening," Betty said quietly. "We have a big day ahead of us tomorrow."

THE FAMILY GATHERED AT THE STEPHAN-STEIN Funeral Home in Long Prairie on Monday, August 26, 1991. It was the day of Marjorie's funeral. The service was planned for 1:00 p.m. at the Long Prairie United Methodist Church where Marjorie had been an active member since 1919.

Marjorie would have loved the beauty of the day. Soft, wispy white clouds dotted the bright blue sky. The sun was brilliant and warm. A gentle breeze made the lush green leaves dance on the tree branches.

The casket bearers followed Mr. Stephan's lead. They wheeled the wooden casket out of the funeral home and lifted it into the shiny black hearse. A procession of cars, filled with family, followed the slow-moving hearse a few short blocks to the United Methodist Church. Reverend Lynn, dressed in a long white robe and carrying a red-covered Bible, greeted Marjorie's family as they followed the pallbearers and Marjorie's casket into the small white church.

The church was full of people. Ushers directed late-arriving guests to folding chairs set in the back vestibule to accommodate the overflow of people. With the afternoon sun shining through them, the colorful stained-glass windows glittered and cast red, yellow, blue, and green vibrant reflections on the wooden pews.

Heat inside the small church was tremendous. Some of the congregation fanned themselves with programs and paperbacked hymnals as they waited to honor Marjorie, their faithful friend. A young woman tried to silence her tiny baby who had started to fuss. After several unsuccessful attempts to quiet the baby, she moved to the back of the church and stood near doors that had remained open to allow any possible breath of air into the church's warm interior.

Reverend Lynn took his place in the pulpit at the right of the cloth-draped altar. Tall white candles on slender gold stems glowed and flickered as he passed them. Reverend Lynn looked over the congregation. He addressed them in a gentle voice, "Family and friends of Marjorie Peterson." Reverently, he paused. "I welcome you today to pray for the soul of our dear, dear departed friend, Marjorie Peterson. Let us bow our heads in prayer."

After a few silent moments, the organist invited the congregation to turn to page 185 in the blue-covered hymnal and join in song as she played, "Nearer, My God to Thee," one of Marjorie's favorite hymns. Readings from the Old Testament and the New Testament followed the hymn.

Reverend Lynn cleared his throat and addressed the gathering again. In a firm voice he said, "The Bible teaches that we, as believers, should be clothed in compassion. Clothe yourselves in compassion. Live in God's example. Live as Marjorie did." Reverend Lynn paused. He wiped beads of sweat from his forehead with a white handkerchief, and then tucked it carefully into the pocket of his vestment. It was very warm in the tiny church. "Wear the garment of mercy," he continued. "Demonstrate concern. Have a tender heart. Be merciful to others, as God has shown us mercy. Wear the garment of kindness. Show a willingness to help those in need. Wear the garment of meekness. Be humble and yet strong of mind. Wear the garment of forgiveness."

"May the Lord help us to be model citizens. Infuse your community with compassion, kindness, humility, and meekness. Show patience. And over all these virtues put on love, which binds them all together in perfect unity. Bear with each other and forgive whatever grievances you may have against one another." His voice became more spirited as he spoke. "Forgive as the Lord forgives you. Let us live in Marjorie's image. Follow her lead, so that we, too, may become citizens of His Heavenly Kingdom." Reverend Lynn raised his arms into the air and looked upward while he paused briefly. "Now, I'd like to invite

Marjorie's family and friends to come forward and share some of their thoughts and special memories of Marjorie."

Frances Moellner rose from the front pew on the right side of the church and apprehensively approached the microphone at the altar. A white handkerchief peeked out between the fingers of her tightly clenched hand. Frances cleared her throat. In the strongest, steadiest voice she could muster she said, "I don't remember exactly when I met Margie. It seems like I've always known her. We were neighbors, you know, for almost forty years. In 1968 Margie and I joined a homemaker group through Todd County Extension. We named our group Prairie Maids." Frances paused while she dabbed her nose with her handkerchief. "Margie and I walked to our homemaker meeting the second Tuesday evening of every month for years. There was a program at every meeting—sometimes we listened to a guest speaker and other times we shared a meal or exchanged recipes. Margie's favorite meetings were the ones with educational programs. I remember one time recently on our walk home, Margie told me how much she enjoyed the program. She said, 'Frances, I might be getting old, but I'm not ready to stop learning.' She loved to learn new things. On the lighter side, at another meeting, we had a program about healthy living. A very fit, young woman in a tight black leotard demonstrated exercises that we should do to stay nimble. She twisted and turned her limbs like a pretzel." Frances put her hands in the air, moved them over her head and loosely imitated the woman she was describing. "Margie and I marveled at the young woman's rubber-like abilities. There wasn't a prayer that either of us could possibly move our creaky, seventy-plus-year-old bodies anything near to the way that she did. We tried our best to mimic her gestures, but we paled in comparison to the young woman. We laughed at ourselves the whole time we walked home. We laughed until we cried." Frances paused. "Those were good times." Tearfully, she added, "I'll miss my dear friend, Margie. I'll especially miss her laughter, but I'll never, ever forget the all the good times that we had."

Frances stepped away from the microphone and walked slowly to her seat in the front pew. Another woman approached the microphone. She patted Frances' shoulder as they passed silently.

The woman adjusted the height of the microphone and cleared her throat. She looked over the congregation as she began to speak. "My name's Darlene Chase. I met Margie at the Ladies Aid Group at this church." Darlene's voice cracked. She paused, took a deep breath and let it out slowly before she spoke again. "Margie joined the Long Prairie United Methodist Church in 1919. In the early 1960s, she became active in the Ladies Aid Group. I don't think she ever missed anything that group did. She gave tirelessly of herself. If you ever came to this church for a wedding or a funeral, you'd always find Margie in the kitchen or the dining hall, preparing or serving the food for one of those occasions. We always put her in charge of the coffee. That ol' coffee pot in the church basement will never make coffee the same again." Darlene brushed the hair from her damp forehead. She continued, "As many of you will remember, Margie's husband, George, didn't share her desire to get out and socialize. He wasn't much for going to church either. I remember one time he told Margie, 'Every time that church bell rings, you run to church. Did you ever think that perhaps you really should've married a minister?'" The congregation broke out in hardy laughter. Darlene walked back to her seat.

Ann walked slowly up the side aisle to the front of the church. She stood still behind the microphone. Pensively, she started to speak, "My name's Ann Zemke. I'm Marjorie's granddaughter." She paused and then thoughtfully said, "I have countless, wonderful memories of my Grandma. It's hard to choose just one to speak about. I talked with my mom, Betty Hengemuhle, as I prepared what I was going to say today. We shared many special stories and memories of Grandma. She was truly a great woman. Just yesterday, I learned that Grandma wrote her autobiography. I had the fantastic fortune to read her life story last night. She wrote a tremendous account of her life journey." Ann pondered what she was going to say next. "I don't know how many of you knew that my grandma was an orphan. At the age of eight in November 1906, she rode an orphan train from the State School Orphanage in Owatonna to Bertha where she was selected from the train depot platform by Grace and Peter Lind. She was never adopted by the Linds, rather she was indentured by them until 1917. One day she took a train to Long Prairie where she found work as a maid and shortly thereafter met George Peterson, her husband of sixty-four years. Although she experienced plenty of bumps and bruises along the way, her kind and gentle spirit was never damaged; rather she grew stronger." Ann took a deep breath and continued, "Grandma had many, many extraordinary qualities. She was an incredibly determined woman who never let adversity get in her way. She always looked for ways to give of herself, and she recognized something good in everyone she met. Most of all, she never, ever uttered a harsh word. Yesterday my mom was helping me prepare what I was going to say about Grandma today. We talked about Grandma's giving spirit. We talked about her kind nature—Grandma never, ever said anything unkind, especially about someone else. Mom and I put our heads together and tried to think of the worst thing that we ever heard Grandma say. We thought long and hard, and finally mom told me about a man and woman in town whom everyone knew. They were rather homely looking people. The couple married. Upon their marriage, Grandma said, 'Isn't that nice, so they didn't ruin two couples.' That was about as shameful as she could muster." Laughter rang through the crowded church. Ann paused as the congregation silenced. "You might laugh, but Mom and I searched long and hard for that feeble instance. It's the only one we could remember. My challenge to myself, and my challenge to you, is to honor my grandma by living in her image. As Reverend Lynn said, have a tender heart. Be merciful to others. Wear the garments that Grandma wore." Ann returned to the second pew of the church.

Reverend Lynn returned to the pulpit. He asked the congregation to bow their heads in prayer. He concluded the service with a final prayer and then invited everyone to a luncheon in the church basement after the internment at the cemetery.

The Ladies Aid group, dressed in colorful embroidered gingham aprons, just like Marjorie wore, worked feverishly in the kitchen and dining hall. They made ham sandwiches on freshly baked buns and served an assortment of gelatin salads and homemade desserts. The coffee pot perked quietly on the kitchen counter.

About the Author

Ann Zemke is a quilt maker and a storyteller. Her passion for quilt making began in 1972, since then, she has handcrafted over 150 unique quilts. Ann tells Marjorie's heartwarming story using the very special quilt that she made in her grandmother's memory, and she has captivated audiences of all types across the United States with this fascinating story and the remarkable quilt it inspired. Ann and her husband live in Blaine, Minnesota.